Shakespearean Intertextuality

Shakespearean Intertextuality

Studies in Selected Sources and Plays

Stephen J. Lynch

Contributions in Drama and Theatre Studies,
Number 86

Greenwood Press
Westport, Connecticut • London

Library of Congress Cataloging-in-Publication Data

Lynch, Stephen J., 1955–
    Shakespearean intertextuality : studies in selected sources and
plays / Stephen J. Lynch.
       p. cm.—(Contributions in drama and theatre studies, ISSN
0163–3821 ; no. 86)
    Includes bibliographical references and index.
    ISBN 0–313–30726–1 (alk. paper)
    1. Shakespeare, William, 1564–1616—Sources. 2. Shakespeare,
William, 1564–1616—Criticism and interpretation. 3. Influence
(Literary, artistic, etc.) 4. Intertextuality. I. Title.
II. Series.
PR2952.L96   1998
822.3′3—dc21   98–22910

British Library Cataloguing in Publication Data is available.

Library of Congress Catalog Card Number: 98–22910
ISBN: 0–313–30726–1
ISSN: 0163–3821

First published in 1998

Greenwood Press, 88 Post Road West, Westport, CT 06881
An imprint of Greenwood Publishing Group, Inc.

Printed in the United States of America

The paper used in this book complies with the
Permanent Paper Standard issued by the National
Information Standards Organization (Z39.48–1984).

10 9 8 7 6 5 4 3 2 1

For Sue
and
for Stephen, Katie, and Hannah

Contents

CHAPTER 1

Introduction: Rethinking Shakespeare's Sources

The concept of the literary source has undergone in recent years an almost infinite expansion to include virtually all expressions of language in a culture: not merely immediate literary or historical influences, but vast arrays of texts (written and unwritten, known and unknown to the author), along with endless networks of linguistic and discursive structures (patterns of thought and logic, commonplace analogies, habitual figures of speech). Shakespeare's plays are no longer seen as based on a few assorted borrowings, but are now seen as interventions in preexistent fields of textuality. The old notion of particular and distinct sources has given way to new notions of boundless and heterogeneous intertextuality.

Perhaps in light of amorphous textuality the old-fashioned source can be newly examined. While recent studies have tended to go further and further afield in search of contextual corollaries and analogues to Shakespeare's plays, the conventional sources have been largely neglected. Yet Shakespeare's immediate source texts can provide especially relevant contextual vantage points from which we can study Shakespeare's plays. Though traditional source studies have tended to see sources as static building blocks that Shakespeare picked over, rearranged, and artfully improved, the sources themselves can be reexamined as products of intertextuality—endlessly complex, multilayered fields of interpretation that Shakespeare refashioned and reconfigured into alternative fields of interpretation. We can reconsider the source texts not merely as raw material for plot and character, but as dynamic and often inconsistent texts involving layers of implicit and subtextual suggestions. For example, in refashioning Lodge's *Rosalynde* into *As*

You Like It, Shakespeare does not merely undermine the Petrarchan and pastoral traditions of the romance, but also undermines and refutes the implicit gender structures of the source text. In refashioning *The True Chronicle Historie of King Leir* into the tragedy of *King Lear*, Shakespeare does not simply reject the explicit Christian setting and happy ending of *Leir*, but engages and responds to the highly reformational and at times Calvinistic tendencies of the source play. In rewriting Greene's *Pandosto* into *The Winter's Tale*, Shakespeare not only adapts the plot and characterization of the source, but consistently counters and refutes the highly euphuistic rhetorical and linguistic structures of the romance. In *Pericles*, Shakespeare adapts the Appolinus story from Gower's *Confessio Amantis*, but also responds to suggestions in the source text about the authority and role of the author. In his revisionary practices, Shakespeare borrows selectively and artfully from his sources, but also reacts against his sources—often by developing and expanding upon contrary suggestions already present in his sources.

My approach may suggest a basic contradiction in that I am invoking the amorphous power of intertextuality while claiming the revisionary skill of a particular author. My attempt, however, is to bridge the gap between traditional assumptions about authorial power and control and poststructuralist claims that authors neither create nor control texts but are themselves products of preexistent cultural discourses. Though I argue for degrees of authorial control, I am not assuming that Shakespeare wrote as a free agent with complete autonomous power over his own revisionary practices. Shakespeare certainly made deliberate and intentional choices: to begin with, he chose (or accepted) particular texts to rewrite and refashion for the stage. Yet virtually all of Shakespeare's revisionary strategies were shaped and influenced by multiple forces beyond authorial control—not only the historical, political, and religious contexts of early modern England, but also the more particular forces that would bear upon a professional playwright, such as contemporary stage practices, generic decorum, audience expectations, the number and quality of available actors, state censorship, and even the geographical locus and marginal cultural status of the theater itself. All such pressures and influences would have come into interactive play in Shakespeare's refashioning of his source materials. Thus I may be placing Shakespeare the author back on stage—but not alone and not always at the center.

Though my focus is on plays and primary sources, I attempt in each chapter to survey the relevant cultural contexts in which these various plays and sources were produced. With the exception of John Gower's *Confessio Amantis*, the sources I consider were roughly contemporary with the plays based upon them, and thus were produced within similar (though not identical) cultural and historical conditions. In each chapter, I begin by exploring how each play and source is embedded and positioned within particular cultural contexts: Elizabethan controversies about gender, conflicting reformational theologies, evolving notions of the role of the author, and disputes about the nature of language. Rather than follow any single approach throughout, I attempt in each chapter to focus on whatever contextual issues seem especially relevant. Shakespeare's revisionary strategies seem wide-ranging and manifold, and what he found interesting or appealing or appalling in each source text seems to vary considerably.

My approach involves a blend of old and new—traditional close attention to the formal aspects of sources and plays, but in light of contemporary critical and theoretical interests. Moreover, my approach is by nature comparative, and, though I risk accusations of bardolatry, I confess up front that in comparison to Shakespeare's sources I consistently find Shakespeare's plays more rich and textually dense—although I would locate Shakespeare's talent for producing such textual complexity in his capacity to exploit to the fullest his primary sources. In his revisionary practices, Shakespeare seems extraordinarily adept at extracting and developing implications that remain underdeveloped in his source texts, while at the same time layering into his plays additional and often oppositional themes and suggestions. In other words, Shakespeare seems consistently to write both with and against his sources, seizing upon and developing suggestions already present in his sources, while complicating his plays with developments that counter and refute his source texts.

Though Shakespeare's rich and subtle plays evolved from a variety of source texts and cultural contexts, his plays also seem wrought with residues and surpluses of signification that cannot fully be accounted for by sources and contexts. In relation to his primary sources, Shakespeare's extraordinarily dense and multilayered plays seem not merely the inevitable products of early modern culture, but distinct expressions of Shakespeare's revisionary skills. Though none of Shakespeare's plays could have been written outside of the shaping influence of various cultural contexts, without Shakespeare's revisionary skills, English Renaissance culture would never have been expressed in such dynamic forms.

With the exception of various studies of Shakespeare's use of Holinshed, Plutarch, and Chaucer, only two book-length studies of Shakespeare's sources have been published: Kenneth Muir's *Sources of Shakespeare's Plays* (1977) and Geoffrey Bullough's *Narrative and Dramatic Sources of Shakespeare* (8 volumes, 1957–75). Muir writes a chapter on each play, identifying various sources and indicating major borrowings and changes made by Shakespeare, while Bullough, in his massive eight-volume work, has assembled virtually all the major sources, but likewise his primary interest is in determining sources and writing general overviews. My interest is not in proving sources, nor in writing general comparisons, but in analyzing, in the light of recent critical and theoretical approaches, the ways in which Shakespeare appropriated and refashioned particular dimensions of his source texts.

In selecting sources for this study I have chosen only sources that Shakespeare used extensively as the primary basis for a play—sources that Shakespeare had closely in mind, if not in hand. I have not selected the sources for *Midsummer Night's Dream*, for example, because they are so diverse that it is extremely difficult to discern at any point what Shakespeare is adapting and transforming. I have chosen, however, the major source for *As You Like It* since most of the key events and characters of the play are already developed in Lodge's *Rosalynde*. Likewise, the main plot of *King Lear,* though shaped and influenced by multiple texts and contexts, is nonetheless extensively based upon the anonymous *King Leir*, a play that in effect provided Shakespeare with a prefabricated rough draft. My interest is not in exploring assorted moments of indebtedness but in analyzing larger, consistent patterns of appropriation, as well as significant patterns of omission (indeed, what Shakespeare left out is often as important as what he put in). Though the sources cannot be reduced to simple templates against which we can measure precise contours of textual difference, the sources do provide highly relevant, prewritten texts that Shakespeare variously adapts, complicates, parodies, refutes, subverts. In Shakespeare's rewriting of his sources, the source texts are not simply used and discarded but linger in the margins of the plays—hypertexts, if you will, of alternative textual possibilities.

CHAPTER 2

Representing Gender in
Rosalynde and *As You Like It*

Like the great Globe itself—built from the dismantled timbers of the earlier Theatre—Shakespeare's plays are not original or autonomous constructions but reconstructions of other constructions (which are themselves reconstructions). *As You Like It* is not an unmediated response to life or love or forests or wrestling techniques, but rather a response to an intertextual network of other texts, particularly and most immediately the primary source text, Thomas Lodge's *Rosalynde* (printed 1590, 1592, 1596, 1598). In refashioning the popular romance as a stage play, Shakespeare rewrites not only Lodge's inscriptions of Petrarchan love and pastoral idealism (as has often been recognized), but Shakespeare also rewrites and re-presents Lodge's inscriptions of gender.[1]

Before examining the various representations of gender in the source and play, we need to consider the historical context in which gender was debated and contested in early modern England—the cultural matrix in which both texts were produced. As recent historical research has shown, Elizabethan England was not a golden age of supreme cultural, political, or gender stability. Despite the many sixteenth-century claims of a natural, divinely ordained social and gender order, such orthodoxies competed within a larger field of controversy and debate about gender—and, for that matter, virtually all human knowledge. By the late sixteenth century, traditional structures and systems of thought, though not overthrown, were radically destabilized. The supremely harmonious and cohesive cosmologies of early Renaissance humanists could no longer be held as certain or absolute in face of such emerging developments as Copernican astronomy, Machiavellian political theory, shifting religious doctrines, geographical exploration and expansion, as well as decades of inflation, widespread unemployment, urban expansion, and emerging mercantile capitalism.[2] Even on the micro-level of legislated dress codes, traditional order could not hold, as wealthier merchants persistently violated Elizabethan sumptuary laws by dressing in the fashion of aristocrats, while—even more alarming—wives of merchants and other city women (who, Jaques complains, bear the "cost of princes on unworthy shoulders" [2.7.76]) proved doubly subversive as they dressed in the fashion of nobility, sometimes male nobility, thus transgressing both traditional class and gender boundaries.[3] Such disruptions of traditional order were compounded by a woman on the throne of England determined to keep the reins of power in her own hands—a divinely sanctioned exception to the rule, as Edmund Spenser tells us, but nonetheless a source of profound cultural anxiety.[4]

As the very foundations of human knowledge were shaken and contested, the highly interrelated assumptions about human gender were contested as well. As evidenced by a series of pamphlets published in the late sixteenth and early seventeenth centuries, the nature and status of women were hotly debated in terms both radical and reactionary. As a general pattern, the debate did not produce increasingly liberal views of women, but rather multiple and conflicting views—often within the same pamphlet. In *Haec-Vir*, for instance (written twenty years after Shakespeare's play but summarizing decades of debate), the bold and aggressive Man-Woman, dressed in masculine attire (complete with sword and spurs), argues vigorously that the differences in dress and manners between men and women are merely the products of "custome," and, she eloquently proclaims, "Custome is an Idiot" (B2).[5] Yet her remarkable proclamation stands not as the definitive or concluding argument of the pamphlet, but as one of several conflicting arguments. At the end of *Haec-Vir*, the Man-Woman suddenly relapses into orthodoxy as she calls for men to resume natural (medieval and chivalric) dress and behavior, and in turn she promises that women will resume natural (silent, chaste, and obedient) femininity.[6]

As such pamphlets indicate, women in Elizabethan England occupied unstable and often indeterminate social positions. Indeed, from the perspective of various Italian and German visitors to London, English women seemed to enjoy remarkable liberty as they drank in taverns and alehouses (Youings 383). Yet, at the very same time, the emerging father-dominated nuclear family, backed by the forces of Protestantism, capitalism, and the nation state, tended to deflect legal and cultural power away from women and increasingly toward men (see Stone 93–146). Thus improvements in the lot of women were often negligible at best. Protestantism, for instance, may have elevated marriage (and implicitly women) above priestly celibacy, but Protestantism also demoted marriage from sacrament to ritual. Moreover, the traditional authority of Catholic priests tended to be appropriated more by fathers and husbands than women. Such conflicting and opposing tendencies created neither a distinct enlargement nor a restriction of women's freedoms but rather a general disruption in their status. Recent studies on the effects of rapid economic change in early modern England suggest that in areas of most rapid change—cities, in particular, and London foremost among them—threats to the status quo from social climbers, especially merchants and their wives, provoked increased attempts at the legal regulation of women (Howard 425–26). Thus a general cultural anxiety about change (the causes of which were at best dimly understood) was focused on the most obvious and easily identifiable upstarts—women. Consequently, the status of women in Renaissance England was both improving and worsening, ironically worsening because it was improving. As city women flexed their economic muscle, they provoked legal measures (such as sumptuary laws) to pressure them into subjection. In early modern London, traditional notions of gender were neither embraced nor overthrown, but anxiously contested and debated in an ongoing struggle among and within texts.

Within this cultural context of an overall destabilization of gender, Lodge and Shakespeare produced their texts (although the impact of such destabilization may have been felt more keenly by Shakespeare, writing in the more volatile and anxious climate of the late 1590s, than by Lodge, writing soon after the heady confidence of 1588). In addition to such cultural controversies, however, we also need to consider the distinctly different professional positions of each author: Lodge as writer of a literary romance and Shakespeare as writer of a stage play. In writing a romance novella, Lodge needed to appeal to those who enjoyed the economic power to purchase books (and could read them)—the fairly well-to-do, those more inclined to feel a vested interest in the status quo. Indeed, Lodge addresses his reading audience as "gentlemen," both in his preface ("To The Gentlemen Readers") and his concluding epilogue ("Heere Gentlemen may you see. . ."). Though the term "gentlemen" was often used inclusively, Lodge nevertheless seems to expect a readership of predominantly male gentry. Shakespeare, on the contrary, writing for the public stage, needed to appeal to a more diverse audience, composed of various social classes, and including large and perhaps increasing proportions of women.[7] Significantly, *As You Like It* ends with an epilogue by a woman character addressed explicitly to women in the audience—an epilogue that may have been the very first spoken by a female character on the Elizabethan stage (see *New Variorum* 301). Though women were not involved in the production of Elizabethan plays, they were certainly involved in the consumption of plays—a position of considerable power and influence that Shakespeare seems to take into account.

Moreover, printed books and performed stage plays occupied different social and geographical positions in sixteenth-century London. Not only were books printed for the relatively elite, but they were marketed within the borders of London, predominantly at the bookstalls in St. Paul's churchyard. Plays, in contrast, were produced for consumption outside the city, in the "liberties," removed from the more rigid legal and social restrictions of London (see Mullaney 26–59). Though both books and plays were subject to state censorship (however loose and inept), in writing for the marginal world of the public playhouse Shakespeare most likely assumed greater thematic license than Lodge.

Rosalynde and *As You Like It* offer competing interpretations of gender, a discursive combat of sorts (though not on a level playing field, since Shakespeare as revisionist always gets the final say). Writing for the socially and sexually diverse audiences of the public stage, in the marginal liberties of the city, and in the more volatile cultural climate of the late 1590s, Shakespeare refashions Lodge's romance, exploiting the complexities of the source text, while radically re-presenting its more traditional constructions of gender.

Like any text, Lodge's romance is not monolithically stable or consistent with itself. Gaps, fissures, and unruly suggestions periodically surface, complicating the overall design, and opening the romance to various interpretations. Yet—if I may put such complications on hold for a while—as a general pattern Lodge writes, or attempts to write, within an orthodox discourse about gender, a discourse steeped in the traditions and formulas of medieval romance. Lodge's men prove active, aggressive, and chivalric, while his women remain relatively static and passive. Women are depicted occasionally as obstacles to male virtue, sometimes as the means towards the attainment of male virtue, but almost always as subservient to the interests of male virtue. The story begins with Sir John of Bourdeaux (counterpart to Sir Rowland de Boys) on his deathbed bequeathing to his three sons their inheritance along with a good bit of manly advice, encouraging them to seek honor, wisdom, and friendship, while warning them to avoid the perils of pride, duplicity, and, above all, women. His longest speech, in fact, is a diatribe against perilous entanglements with women:

> a womans eye as it is precious to behold, so it is prejudiciall to gaze upon; for
> as it affoordeth delight, so it snareth unto death. Trust not their fawning favours, for their loves are like the breath of a man upon steele, which no sooner
> lighteth on but it leapeth of, and their passions are as momentarie as the col-

ours of a Polipe, which changeth at the sight of everie object. . . . [W]omen are
wantons, and yet men cannot want one: and therefore if you love, choose her
that hath her eyes of Adamant. . . and yet my sonnes, if she have all these qualities, to be chast, obedient, and silent; yet for that she is a woman, shalt thou
finde in her sufficient vanities to countervaile her vertues. (162–63)

Sir John's deathbed speech establishes in the very opening pages of the romance a code of gender differences that continues to inform and guide the
narrative. Consistently, the heroic values of honor and male friendship are
implicitly or explicitly upheld, while women (even though "chast, obedient,
and silent") prove distractions from masculine virtue. Lodge may intend a
touch of irony in that the sons find love and find it not so dreadful, but as the
romance develops the heroic values of Sir John, though not uncontested,
continually prevail.

In the stage play, Shakespeare excludes the entire episode, beginning instead with the ensuing sibling rivalry. Though as a playwright Shakespeare
needed to compress the leisurely romance into two hours' traffic of the stage,
the absence of a misogynist starting point produces effects beyond mere dramatic efficiency. Cutting the death scene, Shakespeare overleaps Sir John's
traditional gender configurations of heroic men and subversive women, refashioning the story so that neither sex is rigidly defined by the revered,
authoritative words of a dying patriarch.

In Lodge's text, the chivalric masculinity of Sir John almost immediately
resurfaces in his youngest son Rosader (Orlando). As Sir John "passed the
prime of his youth in sundrie battails against the Turkes" and "was for his
courage chosen the principall of all the Knights of Malta" (160), in like manner Rosader expresses his emergent masculinity through feats of manly
heroism. After enduring years of lowly servitude at the hands of his eldest
brother, Rosader at last finds the courage to assert his will:

I am thine equall by nature, though not by birth; and though thou hast more
Cards in the bunch, I have as many trumps in my hands as thy selfe. Let me
question with thee, why thou hast feld my Woods, spoyled my Manner houses,
and made havock of such utensals as my father bequeathed unto me? (167)

His brother Saladyne (Oliver) responds by ordering his servants to bind
Rosader, and then Rosader, in his newly discovered manliness—"perceiv-
ing his beard to bud" (166)—picks up a garden rake and attacks with such
ferocity that "he hurt some of them, and made the rest of them run away"
(167).

   In refashioning the romance, Shakespeare consistently reduces chivalric and heroic aggression to a bare minimum. Oliver merely strikes Orlando, and Orlando forgoes the garden rake in favor of seizing Oliver by the throat. The status of Orlando's beard is not specified, and in any case does not "bud" with the force of an innately determined chivalry. Orlando's less vigorous masculinity is even suggested in his initial cause for discontent. He is concerned not with his loss of woods and manor houses, but with his stunted education:

> My father charg'd you in his will to give me good education. You have train'd me like a peasant, obscuring and hiding from me all gentleman-like qualities. The spirit of my father grows strong in me, and I will no longer endure it; therefore allow me such exercises as may become a gentleman. (1.1.63–69)

While in the romance the father leaves Rosader a substantial legacy of woods and manor houses (the largest share), along with symbolic tokens of chivalric heroism ("my Horse, My Armour and my Launce" [161]), in the play Sir Rowland bequeaths unto Orlando a legacy more ethereal and refined, a "spirit" more in keeping with the *Book of the Courtier* than the *Song of Roland*. Even his brother cannot help but notice: "he's gentle, never school'd and yet learned, full of noble device, of all sorts enchantingly belov'd" (1.1.157–59). In a revisionary shift of emphasis, Shakespeare represents the hero less in terms of combat skills and more in terms of non-gender-specific moral virtue.

   The rather heavy-handed chivalric virility of the romance can be traced back to Lodge's own source, the *Tale of Gamelyn* (c. 1350). In the anonymous *Tale*, the code of chivalric heroism dictates virtually the entire plot. Gamelyn breaks the neck of a porter and throws him down a well, later breaks the arms and legs of assorted abbots and priors, and finally hangs his brother—along with the judge and the entire jury. Only in the last four lines is there any mention of Gamelyn taking a wife (who remains anonymous). In reworking his primary source, Lodge both reduces the manly brutality and greatly magnifies the role of women, thus rewriting the *Tale* along lines similar to Shakespeare's rewriting of the romance. A glance at the medieval *Tale* also reminds us that even in Lodge's *Rosalynde* gender is not entirely traditional or stable but a revisionary re-presentation of a still earlier representation of gender.[8]

   In the scene of the wrestling match, Shakespeare continues to minimize the manly heroism of the romance. In Lodge, the Norman wrestler not only defeats but kills two sons of a franklin, one by falling upon him with the "weight of his corpulent personage," the other "he threw . . . against the ground so violently, that he broake his neck, and so ended his dayes with his brother" (170). Rosader then enters the list, throwing the Norman to the ground, and falling upon his chest with such force that he kills him: "the Norman yeelded nature her due, and Rosader the victorie" (171). In Shakespeare's play, fatalities are suggested when Le Beau anticipates that the injured opponents will die, but we do not witness their deaths, nor do we know the fate of Charles, who is speechless but alive when carried off stage. Though generic decorum may have required Shakespeare to keep things generally pleasant and more in keeping with the spirit of a comedy, such revisions also seem part of an overall tendency to downplay heroic masculinity. Though Orlando's heroism is clearly demonstrated by his victory—and reinforced by Adam's praise of him as "gentle, strong, valiant" (2.3.6)—the more rigorous heroism that prevails in the romance (and dominates the anonymous *Tale*) rarely surfaces in the play.

In the source text, chivalric heroism continues to resurface as an insistent theme. Even Saladyne, though he schemes and manipulates Rosader into challenging the Norman wrestler, cannot help but acknowledge his brother's surpassing valor:

> thou Rosader the youngest in yeares, but the eldest in valour, art a man of strength and darest doo what honour allowes thee; take thou my fathers Launce, his Sword, and his Horse, and hie thee to the Tournament, and either there valiantlie crack a speare, or trie with the Norman for the palme of activitie. (168)

In the stage play, Shakespeare refashions the tournament into an occasion for anti-chivalric humor: "It is the first time that ever I heard breaking of ribs was sport for ladies" (1.2.129–31). Moreover, Orlando (unlike Rosader) goes off to the wrestling match "disguised" (1.1.120), an emblematic suggestion that heroic masculinity (at least of the rib-breaking sort) is not innate or natural to Orlando but an adopted and artificial pose.

As Lodge's men are active and aggressive, his women are habitually silent and passive. Rosalynde and Alinda (Celia) attend the wrestling match as impressive but entirely passive ornaments of feminine grace and beauty:

> [Rosader] cast his eye upon the troupe of Ladies that glistered there like the starres of heaven, but at last Love, willing to make him as amourous as he was valiant, presented him with the sight of Rosalynd, whose admirable beautie so inveagled the eye of Rosader, that forgetting himselfe, he stoode and fed his lookes on the favour of Rosalynds face. (171)

The episode proceeds according to formula as Rosalynde, like Sidney's Stella, looks on and inspires Rosader to victory: "which glance of Rosalynd so fiered the passionate desires of Rosader" that he "roused himselfe and threw the Norman against the ground" (171). Aside from the invaluable assistance rendered by her eyebeams, however, Rosalynde barely stirs. Even when she rewards Rosader with a jewel, she delivers it not herself but by means of a page.

In the play, Celia parodies the romance by wishing for a "thunderbolt in mine eye" (1.2.205). Yet even though womanly eyebeams prove of little effect, Rosalind seems considerably more active than Rosalynde, delivering the chain personally and taking the initiative a second time when she calls Orlando back to tell him outright, "Sir, you have wrestled well, and overthrown / More than your enemies" (1.2.244–45). Even before she adopts masculine disguise, Shakespeare's Rosalind assumes the traditionally masculine characteristics of power and control.[9]

Though the wrestling scene begins with a clear opposition between the vigorous Orlando and the feeble Rosalind—"The little strength that I have, I would it were with you" (1.2.185–86)—the scene ends with such constructions deconstructed: Orlando stands silent and still as a "lifeless block" (1.2.241), outwrestled by the power of Rosalind. Though Orlando's sudden passivity may fall within the range of traditional Petrarchan lovesickness, his passivity is quite unlike that of Rosader, who suffers no comparable diminishment of manly vigor but instead instantly sets pen to paper and sends a sonnet to Rosalynde.

Such departures from the source text likely served various interests—not the least of which may have been Shakespeare's desire (as a shareholder in the Globe theater) to minimize the number of actors and keep down the payroll. But cuts and revisions could be made in an infinite variety of ways, and consistently Shakespeare makes such adjustments in ways that undermine and subvert the more orthodox constructions of gender in the source text. Heroic masculinity surely finds its way into the play, but its more rigorous forms are displaced from the hero to Charles the wrestler and the tyrannical Duke Frederick. While Lodge's Rosader functions as the definitive essence of manly vigor and prowess, Shakespeare's Orlando symbolically overthrows the brute strength of Charles and then distances himself from the willful tyranny of Frederick as he heads for the political and gender liberty of the forest. Moreover, Shakespeare supplements the stage play with the effeminate character Le Beau, a man (or womanish man) who acts not as an obsequious fop but as an agent of moral virtue, urging Orlando to flee the tyrant Duke.

Shakespeare's proclivity for gender bending is especially evident in his revision of the banishment episode. In the romance, Rosalynde responds to banishment by cleverly adopting a masculine disguise, yet her skill at cross-dressing (though highly suggestive) ultimately tends to endorse traditional gender types. When Alinda expresses dismay at the danger of women traveling unescorted, Rosalynde reacts by playfully scolding her for her lack of traditional feminine wiles:

> Tush (quoth Rosalynd) art thou a woman, and hast not a sodaine shift to prevent a misfortune? I (thou seest) am of a tall stature, and would very well become the person and apparell of a page, thou shalt bee my Mistris, and I will play the man so properly, that (trust me) in what company so ever I come I will not bee discovered; I will buy mee a suite, and have my rapier very handsomely at my side, and if any knave offer wrong, your page wil shew him the point of his weapon. (180)

Lodge's heroine assumes highly conventional gender traits: women are shifty, men are brave. Although Rosalynde manages to "play the man," it is her very femininity—her innate capacity for craft and deception—that enables her to effectively ape masculinity. Ironically, Rosalynde's aptitude for masculine disguise, though potentially subversive, ends up manifesting her essential and God-given feminine nature.

In dramatizing the event, Shakespeare borrows the episode in much of its detail, but develops in Rosalind a more subtle and subversive perspective:

> Were it not better,
> Because I am more than common tall,
> That I did suit me all points like a man?
> A gallant curtle-axe upon my thigh,
> A boar-spear in my hand; and—in my heart
> Lie there what hidden woman's fear there will—
> We'll have a swashing and a martial outside,
> As many other mannish cowards have
> That do outface it with their semblances. (1.3.112–20)

Though Rosalind, like her counterpart, assumes women are naturally fearful, her sense of gender is less fixed and less rigid, since, as she recognizes, men are often just as cowardly even if they dress and act according to cultural codes and expectations. For Rosalind, heroic masculinity is a disguise—not merely for cross-dressing women, but also for men who assume "semblances" of a "swashing and a martial outside." The stage Rosalind exposes heroic and chivalric masculinity as artifice, more style than content, more performance than essence.

The very accouterments of masculinity that Shakespeare's heroine chooses—a "gallant curtle-ax" and "boar-spear"—also seem playfully ironic. In the late sixteenth century, such weapons would seem laughably archaic, demonstrable proof that Rosalind is too much of a lady to have any clear notion of what it means to be a man. Yet, at the same time, such outmoded weapons suggest a parody, not particularly of Lodge (whose heroine chooses a contemporary "rapier") but of the antiquated masculinity of chivalric traditions. Thus Rosalind's curtle-ax and boar-spear comically deflate both women who think they can be men, and men who think they can be men—or, at least, heroic men like the legendary (and thus largely fictional) Roland. In effect, Shakespeare achieves a balanced indeterminacy: not wholly denying gender differences since Rosalind seems unable to assume anything but an absurdly anachronistic masculinity, but not wholly affirming conventional gender differences since such differences seem not essential but historically contingent, expressions of arbitrary and changing fashions (boar-spear one century, rapier the next). While the romance tends to endorse conventional notions of gender, the play swings both ways: exposing conventional gender as mere artifice, while affirming at least some level of innate and natural gender differences.

Throughout the play, Shakespeare parodies and exposes conventionality in virtually all human identities—not merely in masculinity and femininity, but in the conventions of courtiers, fools, lovers, philosophers, shepherds, and melancholics (all seven types). This persistent theme of identity as artifice may have been even more prominent for an Elizabethan audience for whom expressions of identity, especially class and gender identity, could be exceedingly artificial—not merely in the elaborate gestures and ceremonies of the Elizabethan court, but even on the streets of London.

Moreover, the very medium of Elizabethan stage performances, in which boys played women (a practice over which Shakespeare had little or no control), almost inevitably works to expose gender identity as artifice. Order and meaning in gender (as in language) depend upon clear and stable differences, and if such differences are exposed by skilled boy actors as cosmetic and changeable, then all traditional structures of gender—as well as all corollary and interdependent structures of political and class hierarchy—teeter on collapse. No wonder Elizabethan moralists complained so bitterly about the theatrical practices of boys playing women and commoners playing kings (see Jardine 15–17; Briggs 171).

In transferring the heroine from romance to stage play, from ink-on-paper to boy-on-stage, Shakespeare teases out subversive suggestions that are latent but underdeveloped in his source. Seizing upon the plot device of a cross-dressing disguise, Shakespeare reinscribes it in the stage play as a full-fledged theme. Indeed, the cross-dressing disguise may even have been what attracted Shakespeare to the romance to begin with, offering an opportunity to exploit and expand upon highly potent and suggestive developments in the source text.[10]

Lodge's text, however, is not rigorously or monolithically orthodox. As with the cross-dressing disguise, contrary implications periodically surface, and occasionally even the more radical Renaissance perspectives on gender (as in *Haec-Vir*) manage to creep into the text. In one episode in particular, conventional gender comes to the very brink of self-deconstruction. When Rosalynde and Alinda first enter the forest, they discover a poem carved in a tree by the dejected Montanus (Silvius), and Rosalynde, pretending to be Ganimede, proceeds to berate women for their disdainful cruelty: "they delight to be courted, and then they glorie to seeme coy; and when they are most desired then they freese with disdaine: and this fault is so common to the sex..." (181). When Alinda objects—"what mettall are you made of that you are so satyricall against women? Is it not a foule bird defiles the owne nest?"—Rosalynde cleverly replies that such discourses are readily changeable, like clothing:

> Thus (quoth Ganimede) I keepe decorum, I speake now as I am Alienas page, not as I am Gerismonds daughter: for put me but into a peticoate, and I will stand in defiance to the uttermost that women are courteous, constant, vertuous, and what not. (181)

Though her flippant "what not" ensures a playful tone, Lodge's Rosalynde at least momentarily suggests that conventional gender types are not essential truth but merely the contrived fictions of various and conflicting cultural discourses. Yet just as the issue becomes problematic—just as old Sir John's gender-defining authority begins to unravel—the matter is dropped, and its more troubling implications remain undeveloped.

In rewriting the romance, Shakespeare may have read into Lodge more than Lodge wrote, or intended to write, into his text, extracting from such episodes their latent potential. Seizing upon the problematic ironies that linger in the background of the romance, Shakespeare develops and reinscribes such ironies into the foreground of the play. When Shakespeare's Rosalind slips from one mode of discourse to another, she does not leave such discourses intact but instead subjects them to prolonged, subversive humor.

While voicing misogynist discourse about women, Rosalind turns such discourse against itself by means of parodic exaggeration:

> At which time would I, being but a moonish youth, grieve, be effeminate, changeable, longing and liking, proud, fantastical, apish, shallow, inconstant, full of tears, full of smiles; for every passion something and for no passion truly anything, as boys and women are for the most part cattle of this color; would now like him, now loath him; then entertain him, then forswear him; now weep for him, then spit at him. (3.2.396–406)

And there's more: Rosalind warns that women are jealous, clamorous, new-fangled, giddy, prone to inappropriate weeping, inappropriate laughter, and their wanton wits make a habit of exiting out the chimney and into their neighbor's bed (4.1.143–61). By reviewing such an abundance of proverbial female vices, and in such rapid succession, Rosalind does not undermine women, but rather undermines the underminers of women by flaunting the absurd fictionality of such discourse, exposing its status as artificial and rhetorical construct rather than natural fact. Parodying the discourse of misogyny, Rosalind does not foul her own nest, as Celia fears, so much as she fouls the nest of her "old religious uncle" (3.2.337), and, for that matter, the entire antifeminist tradition stretching back to St. Jerome and Aristotle, not to mention Lodge's Sir John of Bourdeaux.[11]

Even in those very moments in the play when Rosalind seems to embrace the conventional femininity of the romance, her habitual posturing and flaunted role-play work to ensure a detached, ironic tone:

> I could find in my heart to disgrace my man's apparel and to cry like a woman; but I must comfort the weaker vessel, as doublet and hose ought to show itself courageous to petticoat. (2.4.4–7)

> Do you not know I am a woman? When I think, I must speak. (3.2.246–47)

> There's a girl goes before the priest, and certainly a woman's thought runs before her actions. (4.1.132–34)

Unlike her romance counterpart, Rosalind remains in the mode of parodic role-play—even when she plays "Rosalind." Weak, crying, garrulous femininity is not the fixed center to which she returns, but instead one more role she enacts. Her closest parallel in the play may be Touchstone, who likewise can never be reduced to one of the roles he plays—whether as melancholic, Petrarchan lover, or courtly dueler. Even his "natural" role as fool becomes merely another role he can readily assume and discard. So, too, Rosalind's periodic assumptions of conventional femininity function not as defining moments of her true essence but rather as additional modes of performance. Like Touchstone, Rosalind does not endorse or privilege one role over another, but sets various and conflicting roles in playful interaction.

The slippery instability of Rosalind's role-play is evident in the sheer number and variety of roles she assumes. While Lodge's heroine flip-flops between male and female roles (Ganimede and Rosalynde), Shakespeare compounds the role-play of his heroine into multidimensional layers: a boy actor who plays a girl who plays a boy who plays a girl, who pushes the envelope even further by enacting a variety of conventional feminine roles—disdainful lady, clamorous shrew, insatiable wanton—as well as a variety of conventional masculine roles—"saucy lackey," "knave," and lover "falser than vows made in wine" (3.2.291–93, 3.5.72–73). Shifting with ease among a dizzying variety of fleeting identities, the stage Rosalind exposes traditional gender types as pure artifice—sets of behavioral codes that can be improvised, altered, and discarded. In the context of the play's persistent concern with "fashion" (a high-frequency word with six occurrences in the text), womanly disdainfulness and wantonness seem no more innate than the latest fashion of petticoat, manly bravado and falseness no more natural than the stylish cut of a courtier's beard.

Along with undermining the natural status of traditional manly heroism in the romance, Shakespeare also excludes from the play several episodes of male bonding scattered throughout the pages of Lodge. When, for instance, Rosader returns from the wrestling match and discovers his brother Saladyne has fled, he proceeds to "frolicke and be merie" with his "crew of boone companions" (173). They "feasted and frolickt it twice or thrise with an upsey freeze" and managed to consume "five tunne of wine" (173). Soon after, Saladyne surprises Rosader in his sleep and has him chained to a post and kept without food for three days, but, with the aide of Adam Spencer, Rosader is set free, and "got a pollax in his hand, and flew amongst them with such violence and fury, that he hurt manie, slew some, and drave his brother and all the rest out of the house" (193). In celebration of their victory, Rosader, Adam, and other "good fellows" then "feasted themselves" (193) in yet another bout of male revelry, until Saladyne returns with the sheriff and twenty-five men, at which time Rosader bursts out of the gates, "wounded manie" (194), and escapes to the Forest of Arden. In the stage play, all of these episodes are excluded, so that Orlando makes only a moderate show of martial heroism, and before entering the forest he enjoys not a moment of male camaraderie.

In cutting the romance down to size, Shakespeare deleted episodes for considerations of genre as well as gender, but along with indecorous brawling and bloodshed Shakespeare consistently excluded episodes of intense male friendship—episodes at the very heart of the romance. The diminished importance of male friendship in the play is perhaps most evident in the changes Shakespeare made to the role of Adam Spencer. In Lodge's romance, the greatest expression of love occurs between Rosader and Adam—between man and man (as Sir John of Bourdeaux would have it). When Adam and Rosader find themselves on the verge of starvation in the forest, the old servant, in a supreme gesture of self-sacrifice, offers his own blood as nourishment to sustain Rosader:

> seeing therefore we can find no foode, let the death of the one preserve the life of the other. I am olde, and overworne with age, you are young, and are the hope of many honours: let me then die; I will presently cut my veynes, &, master, with the warme bloud relieve your fainting spirits: sucke on that till I ende, and you be comforted. (195–96)

Shakespeare follows Lodge by presenting Adam as indeed loyal and generous, but ignores the Christ-like blood offering, thus toning down the love of Adam, making his affections less likely to prevail as a definitive ideal. The relatively peripheral status of Shakespeare's Adam can also be gauged by his eventual fate: while in the romance he remains a major figure even at the end, in the play he simply vanishes. The absent Adam does not merely economize on the staging but reconfigures the priorities of the story, shifting the theme of male friendship from foreground to background.

Similarly, Shakespeare deemphasizes the lengthy and somewhat laborious reconciliation between the two brothers in the romance. In Lodge, Rosader and Saladyne are not only happily reunited but their new-found love takes clear precedence over their attachments to women. After Rosader saves Saladyne from the lion, Adam Spencer praises the brothers for living up to the ideals of their father: "this was the concord that olde Sir John of Bourdeaux wisht betwixt you. Now fulfill you those precepts he breathed out at his death" (220). Their brotherly bond is of such paramount importance that for days Rosader entirely neglects Rosalynde:

> Rosader tooke his brother Saladyne by the hand, and shewed him the pleasures of the Forrest, and what content they enjoyed in that meane estate. Thus for two or three days he walked up and down with his brother, to shew him all the commodities that belonged to his Walke. (220–21)

All this time Rosalynde is left, understandably, "perplexed" and "in a great dumpe" (221). When Rosader finally does return to Rosalynde, he is sharply reprimanded by Alinda for his lapsed performance: "I see well hote love is soone colde" (221). But once Rosader explains the cause for his absence, both women quickly forgive him, and even applaud his brotherly reunion: "Rosader discourst unto them what had hapned betwixt them: which reconcilement made them gladde, especially Ganimede" (221). Though a conflict momentarily surfaces between male friendship and heterosexual love, such tensions are quickly erased from the narrative. Rosalynde voices no complaint, apparently because Rosader has not transgressed the fundamental code of heroic and manly values that underlies the text. Rosader neglects Rosalynde in favor of virtuous devotion to male friendship—a supreme value, even for women.

In refashioning the romance, Shakespeare elevates love for women to a distinctly higher status (perhaps at least partly in response to the apparently growing numbers of women in Shakespeare's audiences). Orlando is far more attentive, and Rosalind far more demanding. Though Orlando proves chronically late for appointments, he is suitably apologetic, and even when wounded by the lioness, he takes the trouble to send his brother with a message. Male friendship surely finds its way from the romance to the stage, but in diminished and muted form, rarely permitted to eclipse a more central and sustained interest in male-female relations.[12]

Though male bonding is generally shifted to the background of the play, it does step to the fore, at least ironically, in the enigmatic and potentially homoerotic friendship between Orlando and Ganymede. In Lodge, homoerotic desire seems suggested in his very choice of the name "Ganimede" (the young boy seduced by Jove), and may even be implicit in the intense and elaborately narrated friendships of Rosader-Adam and Rosader-Saladyne. (Lodge claims in his dedication to have written the romance on a sea voyage—a venture conducive to male friendships and male bonding.) In the play, Shakespeare follows Lodge by adopting the name "Ganymede", but on stage Ganymede is played by a boy actor, complicating enormously the dynamics of the relationship. Thus, when Orlando begs a kiss (which Rosader never does), we cannot be sure whether he is begging a kiss from the boy Ganymede or the girl Rosalind. Indeed, the stage play remains teasingly ambiguous about whether Orlando falls in love with the Rosalind in Ganymede, or the Ganymede in Rosalind, or the androgynous wholeness of Rosalind/Ganymede. In any case, however, while Lodge divides his narrative interests between primary male relationships and secondary male-female relationships, Shakespeare concentrates in the stage play on a single and central hetero-homo-erotic relationship. Unlike the romance, in which male bonding and male-female bonding are kept distinctly separate and unequal, Shakespeare melds and conflates the two, thus—in opposition to Western traditions going back to Plato's *Symposium*—elevating traditionally second-rate heterosexual love to the revered status of male friendship.

Perhaps Shakespeare's most explicit subversion of traditional heroic manliness is when Orlando approaches Duke Senior and company in the forest. Just as the hero begins to act most like his chivalric namesake (Roland), he most nearly makes a fool of himself. His sudden aggressiveness even exceeds that of Rosader in the equivalent episode in the source. When Rosader approaches King Gerismond and his band of outlaws in the forest, he acts with remarkable restraint, graciously requesting food and then proposing sword play only as a means of demonstrating his nobility. He threatens bloodshed only as a last resort:

> Whatsoere thou bee that art master of these lustie squires, I salute thee as graciously, as a man in extreame distresse may; knowe that I and a fellow friend of mine, are heere famished in the forrest for want of foode: perish we must unlesse relieved by thy favours. Therefore if thou be a Gentlemen, give meate to men, and to such men as are everie way worthie of life; let the proudest squire that sittes at thy table, rise & incounter with me in anie honourable point of activitie whatsoever and if he, and thou prove me not a man, send me away comfortlesse. If thou refuse this, as a niggard of thy cates, I will have amongst you with my sword. (196)

Shakespeare rewrites the episode so that Orlando acts more like Rosader than Rosader. Orlando's sudden burst of manly aggression—"Forbear, and eat no more"—is then immediately subjected to the satire of Jaques—"Why, I have eat none yet," "Of what kind should this cock come of?" (2.7.88, 90). The overblown and misplaced heroism of Orlando suggests a parody (in this case not of the gracious Rosader but of the general traditions of chivalric masculinity). Such masculinity proves out of place in Shakespeare's forest, where Duke Senior encourages only Orlando's more refined qualities: "Your gentleness shall force / More than your force move us to gentleness" (2.7.101–02). Orlando's journey from court to Forest of Arden suggests not only a return to the Garden of Eden and the Golden Age, but a return to the more wholesome condition of prefallen, pregendered humanity—the androgynous condition of Adam before the Fall.[13] Accompanied by Adam, Orlando recovers the androgynous Adam in himself—a recovery emphasized in the feminine, nurturing metaphor he uses to describe himself going to the aid of the old man: "like a doe, I go to find my fawn / And give it food again" (2.7.127–28). Whereas Lodge's Rosader travels from court to country with his chivalric masculinity fully intact, Shakespeare's Orlando (though never reduced to a "tame snake" like Silvius [4.3.71]) finds his masculine virtues minimized from the start and refined even further in the greenwood. Indeed, it must be difficult to maintain standards of chivalry in a place where a "wounded knight" can be mistaken for a "dropped acorn" (3.2.232–38).

Yet, as the generally conservative romance lapses into moments of subversion, the more subversive stage play lapses into moments of conservatism. Indeed, at key moments the play seems to come around to reaffirm conventional gender, ironically subverting its own subversive tendencies. For example, Rosalind, despite her skill at aping masculinity, very femininely swoons at the sight of blood, and Orlando has little trouble in manhandling both a wrestler and a lioness. Beneath the variable masquerades of artificial gender types, the play at times seems to point to a solid bedrock of innate gender differences. Yet even these momentary affirmations of natural and innate gender seem somewhat hesitant and tentative, especially compared to the romance. Immediately after Orlando defeats the lioness in an act of Herculean manliness, he responds to brotherly reconciliation with feminine gentleness and sensitivity—"Tears our recountments had most kindly bathed" (4.3.141)—quite unlike Rosader who kills the lion and remains steadfastly heroic, reprimanding his brother for effeminate weeping—"teares are the unfittest salve that anie man can applie for to cure sorowes, and therefore cease from such feminine follies" (218). Moreover, immediately after Rosalind femininely swoons, she repeatedly insists that she "counterfeited" (4.3.167–82); and, of course, she did "counterfeit" in the sense that her swoon was not authentic but fake, an enacted swoon by a boy actor. Just as the play seems to offer some glimpse of an underlying bedrock of nature, the play backs off, exposing its own artificiality. Indeed, the stage play repeatedly flaunts its own status as counterfeit—"an old tale," "a pageant truly played," "in blank verse" (1.2.113, 3.4.50, 4.1.29–30). What the nature of nature may be, precisely, remains stubbornly elusive and indeterminate. The play does not deconstruct conventional gender only to reconstruct gender on more knowing terms, but instead continually deconstructs the very concept of nature, or natural gender, as something that can be articulated or discerned outside the shaping influence of custom and culture. The firm distinction in Lodge's romance between artifice and nature collapses in Shakespeare's play into an all-embracing singularity of artifice. While Lodge offers his text as an artifice about nature, Shakespeare demotes (and promotes) his text as an artifice about artifice. In the stage play, the bedrock of nature always proves elusive, always outside and beyond the range of text and performance.

The intractability of essential nature is suggested repeatedly in the play. Though the Forest of Arden may seem at first a locus of raw nature, where

Duke Senior comes to know feelingly what he is, we quickly discover that though he sleeps in a cave, he eats at a table (artifice), perhaps at the head of a table (more artifice), and the natural forest ceases to be natural the moment he arrives and displaces the native deer. Even Corin, the "natural philosopher," disrupts the natural world by making a living through the "copulation of cattle" (3.2.30, 78), and, of course, Touchstone goes nowhere without his clock. Indeed, there is no getting outside of human artifice.

At every turn, the play exposes the artificial, not only in gender and portable clocks but in the myriad and inexhaustible range of things human: court manners, cosmetics, beard fashions, deer killing, sheep breeding, friendship feigning, tree carving, not to mention body posture—"bear your body more seeming, Audrey" (5.4.68–69). The play's wildly proliferating discourse on customs and conventions suggests that indeed "All the world's a stage" (2.7.138), including the melancholic pose of proclaiming all the world a stage. Human identities (Seigneur Love, Monsieur Melancholy, Monsieur Traveler) are inevitably performative and theatrical, not the order of God but of man, not nature but culture.

Language itself proves the master artifice. As Touchstone proclaims, a man can swear by his honor that the pancakes are good and the mustard bad, and yet not be forsworn—even if the pancakes are not good and the mustard not bad. Language for Touchstone is a sport, an exercise of cleverness and wit, a fabrication detached from nature and truth. The more elegant and figurative the language, the more fictional: "the truest poetry is the most feigning" (3.317–18). The referential gap between language and truth in the play widens into a comic abyss in the case of Silvius, who directs his affections at a purely fictional and discursive construct (while Lodge's Montanus, by contrast, pines for a Phoebe who by all reports is indeed beautiful—thus in the romance language and truth remain closely allied). Though Orlando is less delusional than Silvius, and Rosalind more keen-witted than Orlando, a troubling irreconcilability between language and truth is never resolved in the play. Human truth, whether of pancakes or of gender, is not discovered in the world but constructed in the artifices of language.

The radicality of Shakespeare's play, however, is enclosed within its own limits. Though Shakespeare may seize upon all that Lodge offers as nature, reinscribing it as artifice, Shakespeare preserves intact the very traditional notion of an art/nature binary as a conceptual lens through which human artifice can be discerned. The entire conceptual structure of the play thus rests upon the presupposition of "nature" as a standard by which "artifice" can be exposed and revealed. Rather than deny nature, Shakespeare's text implicitly upholds and affirms the concept of nature, if only by an indirect process of negating all that is not nature (a kind of *via negativa*, akin to Thomas Aquinas' attempt to delineate the qualities of divine nature by means of negating all qualities that are not divine). Shakespeare's implicit (and perhaps unconscious) affirmation of nature would likely have had special appeal in the anxious cultural climate of the late 1590s—offering an implicit reassurance that all the philosophic, economic, and gender flux of the age may be merely in the domain of human artifice, while an essential and fixed nature may exist after all, although quite beyond the reach of language and stage representation.

The artificiality of gender in the play comes into sharper focus when viewed in relation to the most prominent artifice in both the source and the play—Petrarchan love. As a general pattern in Lodge's narrative, Petrarchan love and natural love happily coexist as untroubled allies. Indeed, the artifices of Petrarchan language encounter only minor setbacks in conveying the truth of natural love. Though Lodge occasionally speaks of art and nature as though they were at odds—"nourture and art may doo much, but that *Natura naturans* which by propagation is ingrafted in the heart, will be at last perforce predominant" (164)—such thematic asides fail to square with the overall developments in the narrative since the essential "nature" that prevails proves virtually identical to "art." As natural masculinity in the romance proves indistinguishable from traditional chivalric masculinity, so natural love proves none other than Petrarchan love.

In rewriting the romance, Shakespeare does not merely undermine the Petrarchanisms of Lodge, but undermines the underlying gender structures upon which such Petrarchanisms are founded. Moreover, Shakespeare does not simply write against the textual grain of the romance, but develops and expands upon contrary suggestions and implications already present in the source text. The romance does not wait around ten years to be undermined by the play, but rather proves quite competent in undermining itself.[14]

Though Lodge may intend to present love and gender within traditional bounds, more radical viewpoints repeatedly surface in the text, complicating and at times sabotaging the overall design. In the course of examining her lover, for example, Lodge's Rosalynde gives voice to highly skeptical, anti-Petrarchan perspectives (although anti-Petrarchanisms are also conventional and well-established even in Petrarch). On one occasion she questions Rosader about his beloved Rosalynde, and he unknowingly replies: "It is shee, O gentle swayne, it is she, that Saint it is whom I serve, that Goddesse at whose shrine I doo bend all my devotions: the most fairest of all faires, the Phenix of all that sexe, and the puritie of all earthly perfection" (201). In response, Rosalynde cleverly turns the tables on him by contrasting her earth-bound self to his imagined deity: "Beleeve me (quoth Ganimede) either the Forrester is an exquisite painter, or Rosalynde faire above wonder: so it makes me blush, to heare how women should be so excellent, and pages [Rosalynde disguised as Ganimede] so unperfect" (203). In a moment of splendid irony, Rosalynde effectively exposes the rhetorical excesses of a lover who can detect no such divine qualities in the flesh and blood that stands before him. The irony is carried even further as Rosader describes Ganimede as rather plain-looking in comparison to his Platonic ideal: "Truly (gentle page) thou hast cause to complaine thee, wert thou the substance: but resembling the shadow, content thy selfe" (203). Rosalynde then goes on to suspect self-absorbed affectation in her lover, fearing that he may prove one of "these Ovidians" who "onely have their humours in their inckpot" and would prefer to "passe away the time heere in these Woods with writing amorets, than to be deeply enamoured" (208). She even suggests that Rosader's imagined ideal may exist only as a cosmetic fabrication: "if boyes might put on their [women's] garments, perhaps they would proove as comely" (203). As minor-league deconstructionist, Lodge's Rosalynde does much of Shakespeare's work for him—playfully exposing Petrarchan ideals as purely discursive and contrived fictions.

In the romance, however, such potent and cutting remarks remain relatively infrequent and subdued, expressions of a mere holiday humor from which the text quickly recuperates. Despite her many comic jabs and even a few knock-down punches at Petrarchan conventions, Lodge's Rosalynde soon revives those very conventions and clings to them as the definitive standards by which she evaluates the love of Rosader. Once she has tested his mettle, she concludes that he will prove a worthy lover so long as he can maintain fidelity to Petrarchan ideals: "if you be true and trustie, ey-paind and hart-sicke, then accursed bee Rosalynde if shee proove cruell: for Forrester (I flatter not) thou art woorthie of as faire as shee" (208). Appropriately, the love game in the romance is pursued merely as a pastime, not a cure, for Rosader needs no cure at all. His Petrarchan ideals prove the right ideals, apparently the only available ideals. Though Rosalynde laughs and criticizes, she ends up disregarding her most troubling and incisive remarks, and happily proceeds to embrace Rosader's Petrarchan love as supreme. At that point, about midway through the narrative, their relationship plateaus. (Indeed, much of the remaining narrative seems merely playful repetition, as Lodge goes on to duplicate the process with Saladyne/Alinda and Montanus/Phoebe). Though Petrarchan discourse begins to unravel in the holiday humor of Rosalynde's love test, Lodge soon reedifies such discourse as a definitive and stable ideal, a secure frame of reference—not mere artifice but the true essence of nature.

In refashioning Rosalynde into Rosalind, Shakespeare appropriates and expands upon suggestions already present in the source text. But while Rosalynde briefly tests and taunts her lover, Shakespeare's heroine persists in the mode of holiday humor, relentlessly and continually exposing love and gender conventions as rhetorical fictions. Unlike her predecessor, the stage Rosalind does not quickly retreat from a position of skepticism. She never finds in Orlando even one of the conventional marks of a true lover:

> A lean cheek, which you have not; a blue eye and sunken, which you have not; an unquestionable spirit, which you have not; a beard neglected, which you have not. (3.2.364–67)

Though many of Roselind's cutting remarks can be traced to Lodge, her irony in the play is more biting and sustained, capable of inflicting damage beyond easy or full recuperation. While in the romance Petrarchanisms eventually prevail as definitive truth, in the discursive combat of the play no single mode of discourse emerges as a stable and secure frame of reference. Shakespeare does not simply turn the romance on its head, demoting Petrarchanisms while promoting anti-Petrarchanisms. On the contrary, even Rosalind's most brilliant deflationary retorts—"Men have died from time to time, and worms have eaten them, but not for love," "men are April when they woo, December when they wed" (4.1.100–02,140–41)—function not as declarations of bedrock truth, but as hyperbolic rhetorical flourishes. (Surely some man has died for love; surely some man was December even when he wooed.) Shakespeare destabilizes both the rhetoric of Petrarchan love and the rhetoric of anti-Petrarchan love. Pitting opposing discourses together in playful interaction, Shakespeare does not privilege one mode of discourse over another, nor assume some Aristotelian middle ground, but exposes all such discourses as rhetorical fictions. While Lodge writes (or attempts to write) within a singular discourse that can be taken (or mistaken) for nature, Shakespeare teases out of Lodge's text multiple, heterogeneous strata, creating fields of discursive combat in which no single discourse prevails but all are denaturalized and exposed as artifice. While the romance tends to minimize and subordinate discursive contradictions, the stage play activates, and keeps activated, multiple and conflicting dimensions of discourse.

Toward the end of the play, however, Shakespeare seems to take another turn back toward the conventional. Moments after Orlando leaves stage, Rosalind suddenly adopts the very language of Petrarchan love: "I cannot be out of the sight of Orlando. I'll go find a shadow and sigh till he come" (4.1.207–09). Yet even here a critical difference between Rosalind and Rosalynde remains: while Lodge's heroine embraces Petrarchan language as the truth of nature, the stage Rosalind voices such sentiments in a mode of self-conscious hyperbole, adopting such conventions while flaunting their conventionality (and if Rosalind should fail to undermine her own lapse into conventionality, Celia serves as backup: "And I'll sleep"). Unlike the romance Rosalynde, the stage Rosalind resorts to the language of Petrarchan love only as a provisional and self-consciously artificial means to express her affections for Orlando—a provisional acceptance of conventions of love that sets the tone for her problematic acceptance of conventions of gender and marriage at the end of the play.

In the play at large, various conventions undergo a similar process of exposure followed by ironic, provisional acceptance. Primogeniture, for instance, appears in the opening scene not as the law of nature but merely as the "courtesy of nations." Yet, however unjust for Orlando (especially in view of the romance in which young Rosader inherits the largest share), the play comes around to reaffirm primogeniture in the final scene when Duke Senior restores the elder brother Oliver to his father's lands. Similarly, conventions of pastoralism may seem obliterated in Act 2 but are suddenly reestablished in Act 5 when Duke Frederick is "converted" after barely setting one foot in the forest.

As the play draws to a close, conventional gender seems likewise restored. Rosalind and Orlando may have been like "co-mates and brothers in exile" (2.1.1), but as Rosalind prepares for marriage, she readily submits to the conventional family and political hierarchies that attend upon it. Her submission is testified by her remarkable silence in the final scene. Though she and Celia were "from their cradles bred together" (1.1.104) and though their love has been "dearer than the natural bond of sisters" (1.2.267), their imminent separation is accepted without any comment and apparently without any hesitation. As Louis Montrose remarks, "Solutions to the play's initial conflicts are worked out between brother and brother, father and son—among men" (52). In the final scenes, Rosalind uses her autonomy and power only to select who shall dominate her. As she sheds her masculine disguise and the power that accompanied it, she willingly engages in a double submission to the patriarchal order of father and husband: "To you [Duke] I give myself, for I am yours. / To you [Orlando] I give myself, for I am yours" (5.4.115–16). As Peter Erickson remarks, "She is the architect of a resolution that phases out the control she has wielded and prepares the way for the patriarchal status quo" (25). In effect, Rosalind arranges a ritual of exclusion that excludes her.

Orlando likewise moves towards a recuperation of conventional gender near the end of the play. The lioness episode in particular seems to signify a recovery of heroic and Herculean masculinity. While Lodge's Rosader defeats a male lion, Orlando confronts and overcomes a doubly feminine threat: a "lioness with udders all drawn dry," and a female snake, "her head nimble in threats approached" (4.3.115,110). Though the lioness may allegorically suggest the sin of Pride or Wrath, and the snake would almost inevitably suggest the temptation and Fall of Man, the creatures also pose a distinctly feminine threat to Orlando. Indeed, in the stage play the lioness is directly linked to Rosalind: as the lioness wounded his arm, Rosalind "wounded" his heart (5.2.22–24). Allegorically, in overcoming the female beasts, Orlando seems to overcome the threatening power of femininity—both in Rosalind and in himself. After a low ebb, Orlando's heroic masculinity stages a comeback. He reassumes traditional masculine gender traits, preparing for a recuperation of the traditional patriarchal order in the final scene.

Yet, however much the play moves towards a restoration of conventional gender and patriarchy, a final look at Lodge's romance suggests that the radical implications that surface throughout the play are not so securely contained within the orthodox framework of the ending. Compared to the play, the romance ends with conventionality winning the day with a considerably greater show of force. Indeed, it is in Lodge's romance, more than in Shakespeare's play, that the recuperative and conservative emphasis of Montrose and Erickson seems best suited.

In Lodge, patriarchy is restored not merely by a series of marriages, but by a full revival of chivalric and heroic values in a most appropriate setting—warfare. It is in the romance, more than in the play, that the essentially conservative spirit of holiday is evoked, what C. L. Barber calls the "misrule which implied rule" (*Festive Comedy* 10). After the multiple marriages (arranged not by Rosalynde but by her father), the new husbands and wives engage in a playful, and distinctly short-lived, holiday reversal of roles: "Dinner was provided, and the tables beeing spread, and the Brides set downe by Gerismond, Rosader, Saladyne and Montanus that day were servitors" (253). The festive role reversal, however, is soon reversed as the third brother, Fernandyne, arrives to urge his brothers to turn from the frivolity of love to the serious business of war:

Although (right mightie Prince) this day of my brothers mariage be a day of mirth, yet time craves another course: and therefore from daintie cates rise to sharpe weapons. And you the sonnes of Sir John of Bourdeaux, leave off your

amors & fall to armes, change your loves into lances, and now this day shewe
your selves as valiant, as hethertoo you have been passionate. . . . [s]hewe your
selves as hardie souldiers as you have been heartie lovers: so shall you for the
benefite of your Countrey, discover the Idea of your fathers vertues to bee
stamped in your thoughts, and prove children worthie of so honourable a par-
ent. (255)

The concluding battle between the forces of Gerismond and Torismond
neatly rounds out the code of heroic values that continually informs the narrative. Sir John's deathbed desires are at last fully realized as his sons join together in a supreme bond of chivalric brotherhood. Sir John essentially
returns in the voice of the third brother to rouse Rosader and Saladyne to
complete their manhood on the battlefield. Appropriately, the romance
draws to a close with the men (Adam Spencer included) duly rewarded for
their martial heroism and success: Rosader is made heir apparent, Saladyne
restored to his father's lands, Fernandyne made Principal Secretary, Montanus made Lord of the Forest, and Adam Spencer made Captain of the King's
Guard. Lodge concludes his narrative with an epilogue to his "Gentlemen"
readers—an epilogue that is perhaps most revealing for what it does not include:

Heere Gentlemen may you see . . . that such as neglect their fathers precepts,
incurre much prejudice; that division in Nature as it is a blemish in nurture, so
tis a breach of good fortunes; that vertue is not measured by birth but by action; that yonger brethren though inferiour in yeares, yet may be superiour to
honours; that concord is the sweetest conclusion, and amitie betwixt brothers
more forceable than fortune. . . . (256)

There is no mention of women. They are erased from the narrative, displaced
by things more important.

Shakespeare's play ends not with an epilogue to men about men, but an
epilogue to women by a woman—an epilogue that, as Rosalind remarks,
breaks the "fashion" of masculine epilogues. It is, moreover, a particularly
troublesome epilogue since Rosalind keeps changing sexes: beginning as a
"lady," acknowledging herself as a man ("If I were a woman"), and mutating
back into a woman as she/he performs a feminine curtsy. Instead of the confident and secure gender roles that forcefully reassert themselves in Lodge,
Shakespeare's play ends with a final gesture of wavering instability.[15] (The
nimble feminine snake, we should recall, was never quite eliminated in the
play: she slipped off into the forest intimidated but in good health, and, in a
sense, returns in the feminine epilogue.)

In cutting the episode of the final battle—along with the various heroics of Rosader, as well as Saladyne's valiant rescue of the women from a band of villains—Shakespeare offers on stage a restoration of patriarchy that is distinctly less pervasive and less deterministic than that of the source text. As the masculinity of Orlando is not defined by feats of heroism, the resurgent patriarchy of Duke Senior is not defined by the values of chivalric warfare. While the romance moves full circle from conventional chivalric heroism back to conventional chivalric heroism, the play moves through too much gender turbulence to simply return to the status quo. What is done, as Lady Macbeth says, cannot be undone.

The end of Shakespeare's play points not to a restored but a reformed patriarchy. The forest serves not as a mere holiday reprieve from the social and gender constraints of the court, but as a liminal space of imaginary freedom in which the values that underlie the court are playfully exposed and skeptically interrogated. What the reformed court might be remains undefined and undetermined. There is no Act 6—at least not on stage.

Though Shakespeare's Rosalind may indeed orchestrate a return to convention, she does so in a context of far less rigid and imposing values. Her conservative turnabout is qualified by the play's persistent exposure of all human behaviors and institutions as inevitably artificial. The marital and political order Rosalind so willingly accepts is not the immutable, divinely sanctioned order of the source text, but an order represented as cultural construct—as contingent and relativistic as the various customs of court and country.

Though the play's complex resolution, or rather irresolution, is never voiced by the silent Rosalind, it is addressed obliquely by the never-silent Touchstone as he launches into his lengthy dissertation on conduct books and dueling conventions (which conveniently gives Rosalind time to change into her wedding dress). As Touchstone explains, the elaborate conventions of dueling (though laughably absurd) can serve the worthy purpose of saving one's neck: "Your If is the only peacemaker; much virtue in If" (5.4.101–02). For Touchstone, as for the Man-Woman in *Haec-Vir*, custom may be, indeed, an idiot—but an indispensable idiot. Touchstone's speech implies that all such conventions (including those of gender, marriage, and politics) may be artificial and contingent but nevertheless necessary for shaping inchoate and potentially hazardous life into something orderly and liveable. Like Touchstone's eagerness to live by the conventions of dueling, Rosalind's submission to conventions of gender suggests not a sanctification of traditional values, but a provisional acceptance of such values within an expanded, relativistic, and skeptical vision of cultural possibilities. The various radical implications in the play may be resolved within the framework of an orthodox comic ending, but the resolution and sense of closure are not as complete or absolute as in the romance. Rosalind, unlike Rosalynde, embraces the conventional role of silent, chaste, and obedient wife as she embraces conventional Petrarchanisms—not as final truth but as provisional role-play, not the order of God's nature but of human culture.

Yet Shakespeare does not abandon the conservative ending of the source text so much as he overlays it with alternative endings. While Lodge offers his audience of book-buying gentlemen an ending in which conventional gender (after some holiday foolery) is firmly restored, Shakespeare offers his more heterogeneous public-playhouse audiences an irresolute multiple ending—both conservative and radical. Shakespeare reinscribes Lodge's ending in a fashion akin to the discourse of skepticism so prevalent in the anxious and uncertain England of the late 1590s. A similar pattern of radical interrogation followed by provisional acceptance can be seen in the highly influential essays of that premiere Renaissance skeptic, Montaigne. In the "Apology for Raymond Sebond," Montaigne argues that all forms of human knowledge are inevitably contrived fictions, cosmetic masks imposed upon the elusive face of nature:

> Just as women wear ivory teeth where their natural ones are lacking, and in place of their real complexion fabricate one of some foreign matter; as they make themselves hips of cloth and felt, and flesh of cotton, and in the sight and knowledge of everyone, embellish themselves with a false and borrowed beauty; so does science (and even our law has, they say, legitimate fictions on which it founds the truth of its justice). . . . As also, for that matter, philosophy offers us not what is, or what it believes, but the most plausible and pleasant thing it forges. (401)

Yet Montaigne, like Rosalind, does not expose artifice merely to toss it to the wind, but ironically to embrace it, though from a more self-conscious and knowing perspective. Montaigne resolves to follow tradition by practicing the old religion and favoring the old astronomy, though not as the way of nature or absolute truth but as a provisional means of rendering human life some measure of order and cohesion. In like manner, the remarkably radical Man-Woman in *Haec-Vir*, after proclaiming custom an idiot, comes round to embrace that very custom as she offers to resume conventional femininity by exchanging her masculine attire for the feminine attire of the Womanish Man:

Be men in shape, men in shew, men in words, men in actions, men in counsell, men in example: then will we loue and serue you; then will wee heare and obey you; then will wee like rich Iewels hang at your eares to take our Instructions. (C3)

Like Montaigne and the Man-Woman, Rosalind will have her cake and eat it too—radically destabilizing convention and conservatively embracing convention.

Louis Montrose sees the play as not merely reflecting but actively intervening in social problems of the late sixteenth century, particularly problems that resulted from the custom of primogeniture. Montrose argues that the play provides "collective compensation" and "wish-fulfillment fantasies" for the multitudes of younger brothers who, like Orlando, found themselves deprived of fortune and means (53). Indeed, a contemporary of Shakespeare, Thomas Wilson, used a rather colorful metaphor to describe a younger brother's inheritance as "that which the catt left on the malt heape" (qtd. in Palliser 65). I would argue, however, that Lodge's romance would have served equally well in providing fantasy fulfillment for younger brothers (placing Rosader, like Orlando, on the fast-track to Dukedom), and that the compensation offered by Shakespeare's play extends beyond frustrated younger brothers to include a wider spectrum of the audience—especially the women Rosalind addresses in her epilogue.

The social problems of city women in late sixteenth-century London were as critical and as much in the public eye as the plight of younger brothers. Like displaced young men, city women occupied highly precarious and unstable positions in Elizabethan culture. They enjoyed the freedoms offered by a thriving urban life, such as drinking in taverns and alehouses (and attending productions of *As You Like It*), but at the same time their freedoms were also restricted by increased legal regulations and by strong patriarchal tendencies in both Protestantism and the emerging nuclear family.

In *As You Like It*, Shakespeare intervenes in the cultural tensions and contradictions produced by the troubling and indeterminate status of women in Elizabethan England. Perhaps one way in which the play appealed to Elizabethan audiences was in mediating between such tensions. The more orthodox and conservative playgoers could derive pleasure by watching traditional gender playfully exposed but never quite overthrown, and in the end restored and recuperated—thus containing women within an orthodox cultural space. And yet upstart women and their sympathizers could find pleasure in the way the play insistently exposes and demystifies such orthodoxies, recuperating them on a decidedly lower plane, removed from the exalted status of divinely sanctioned nature—thus effectively expanding the space in which women are contained. (Moreover, virtually everyone could find reassurance in the play's implicit affirmation of some elusive realm of stable "nature"—however undefined and undefinable.) In the midst of widespread cultural destabilization and resultant anxieties and psychic disruptions, Shakespeare refashions the more orthodox gender structures of his source text, offering Elizabethan playgoers a cohesive re-presentation of gender, conservative enough and yet flexible enough to suit a maximum range of taste, and in that way, along with many others, most everyone (including Shakespeare the poet and Shakespeare the stockholder) gets it as they like it.

Notes

1. Previous studies of *Rosalynde* and *As You Like It* have tended to concentrate almost exclusively on the various treatments of love and pastoralism in the two texts. See Muir 125–31; Bullough 2: 143–57; Mincoff 78–89; Pierce 167–76; and Berry 44–51. Muir and Bullough provide episode-by-episode comparisons of the play and source, Mincoff analyzes structural differences, Pierce concentrates on the anti-Petrarchan effects of Shakespeare's addition of Jaques and Touchstone, and Berry studies Shakespeare's transformation of Rosalynde into Rosalind.

2. For a recent survey of the disintegration of the medieval worldview, see Dollimore 83–108, 153–81.

3. For studies of cross-dressing in Elizabethan England, see Howard 418–40 and Jardine 141–68. The perceived threat to the social structure posed by the unconventional dress of Elizabethan women can be discerned particularly in the sumptuary legislation of the 1570s, which began to treat women as a distinct and separate group (see Newman 120–21). Another effect, as well as further cause, of destabilization in the Elizabethan social structure can be seen in the growing tendency of aristocrats to marry below their class, usually into families of wealthy merchants: "Between 1485 and 1569 over half the peers and male heirs of peers married within the peerage, but between 1570 and 1599 the proportion fell to a third" (Palliser 63).

4. See *Faerie Queene* 5.5.25. I do not mean to suggest that Queen Elizabeth deliberately undermined conventional notions of gender. On the contrary, Elizabeth never appointed a woman to a position of power in her administration, and in fact often derided her own sex, strategically exploiting traditional views of women in order to elevate herself as a miraculous exception to the rule. As Christopher Haigh remarks, Elizabeth wanted to be seen as an "adored goddess or an untouchable virgin, never as a mere female" (*Elizabeth I* 19). Lisa Jardine also sees Elizabeth as exalted "in spite of her sex," but goes on to argue that the cumulative effect of "half a century of iconographic effort to convert a female monarch to 'manly'

strength appears . . . for a fleeting moment to have dislodged the weight of traditional assumptions." Jardine cites as evidence Shakespeare's *Phoenix and the Turtle* in which conventions of gender are inverted: the female phoenix is active and vigorous, the male turtle passive and nurturing (194–95).

5. The claim that female subordination is merely a human custom, rather than natural or divine law, was widely stated in the Renaissance. See, for example, Agrippa of Nettesheim, *Of the Nobilitie and Excellencie of Womankynde* (English translation, 1542): "And thus by these lawes the women being subdewed as it were by force of armes, are constrained to give place to men, and to obeye theyr subdewers, not by no naturall nor divyne necessitie or reason, but by custome, education, fortune, and a certayne tyrannicall occasion" (qtd. in Jordan 124–25).

6. I would add that the ideal of the fully subordinate wife was more of a Renaissance fantasy about the medieval past than a factual reality of the medieval past. Indeed, aristocratic medieval women often enjoyed greater social and legal power than their Renaissance descendants. See Jordan 11–21 and Kelly 19–50.

7. For evidence of increasing numbers of women in Renaissance theater audiences, see Gurr 55–64 and Levin 165–74. Levin acknowledges the absence of firm evidence for estimating the numbers of women in Renaissance theater audiences, but observes that when Shakespeare addresses his audiences in epilogues, he tends to favor gender-neutral terms such as "gentles" or "fair beholders," and, unlike some dramatists, Shakespeare never speaks only to men. Moreover, in the 1590s prefaces and epistles in printed playbooks tended to shift from the early formula, "To the Gentlemen Readers" (*Tamburlaine*, 1590), to more neutral phrases such as "To the Reader" or "To the Courteous Reader."

8. For an overview of the *Tale of Gamelyn*, see *New Variorum* 483–87. Though the *Tale of Gamelyn* does not seem a direct source for *As You Like It*, one line in the play may suggest that Shakespeare had some familiarity with the medieval story: Celia remarks that the wrestling contest sounds like "an old tale" (1.2.113).

9. As Margaret Beckman observes, even Rosalind's wit can be considered masculine: "Her puns, witticisms, and paradoxes first of all show her as a 'masculine' intelligence, not because Shakespeare thought women incapable of wit, but because to be witty is to be able to control others and to lead them, as Rosalind leads Orlando" (49). I would add, however, that manipulative wit seems the strategy of the underdog (with Rosalind as a Renaissance version of Brer Rabbit), though for Rosalind (and Brer) wit becomes the means for a temporary reversal of power relations.

10. Harold Bloom might call this a "revisionary swerve," a willful misreading of the precursor text (*Anxiety* 19–45).

11. Though Rosalind focuses on the psychological, not physiological, deficiencies of women, her casual equation of "boys and women" may parody ancient assumption that women, like boys, are anatomically underdeveloped or embryonic men. Renaissance medical treatises, following the authority of Galen, claimed that

the bodies of women lack sufficient "heat" so that their genitals never fully develop and consequently remain on the inside instead of evolving, as in men, fully and outward. For an analysis of this concept in relation to *Twelfth Night*, see Greenblatt 77–83.

12. Peter Erickson argues, on the contrary, that in *As You Like It* male values consistently reign supreme, especially in the "pattern of male reconciliation preceding love for women" (30). Similarly, Janet Adelman sees the play as presenting an "all male Eden" in which the society of Duke Senior "keeps its distance from women—in fact promises fulfillment without women" (84–85).

13. As Robert Kimbrough remarks, "The original wholeness of each human as Man, Woman, and Androgyne in Plato's *Symposium* and the tradition of Adam as androgynous were known throughout medieval and Renaissance Europe" (20).

14. Contrary to my argument, the critical consensus has been that Lodge never tests his conventions. As C. L. Barber comments, "Lodge, though he has a light touch, treats the idyllic material at face value. He never makes fun of its assumptions, but stays safely within the convention" (*Festive Comedy* 227; also see Pierce 170).

15. Related interpretations of the epilogue can be found in Belsey 180–81 and Rackin 36.

CHAPTER 3

English Reformations in *King Leir* and *King Lear*

Shakespeare's *King Lear* has often been interpreted as a play in which Christian themes and patterns are evoked, but in the end brutally and profoundly negated.[1] Yet this critical tendency to configure *King Lear* in terms of an opposition between Christianity and the forces of anti-Christianity (atheism, radical humanism, empiricism, skepticism, philosophic materialism) may evolve from an inadequately historicized view of Christianity in early modern England. As recent historical research has indicated, the most powerful and persistent tensions in reformational England were often not between religion and non-religion, but rather within religion—within various, contrary, highly contested interpretations of Christianity (see Duffy; Scarisbrick; and Haigh, *Reformations*). In light of recent historical research, the powerful sense of negation in *King Lear* seems directed not at some generalized Christianity, but rather at the distinctly reformational and Calvinistic tendencies of the primary source text, the anonymous *True Chronicle Historie of King Leir and His Three Daughters* (c. 1590, printed 1605).

Though *King Leir* and *King Lear* are stage plays, not theological treatises, both texts emerge from and appeal to intertextual networks of theological values and assumptions. The authors of both plays prudently avoid explicit involvement in such explosive (and censored) issues as papal authority, veneration of saints, purgatory, and transubstantiation. Yet neither text is theologically neutral, but rather positioned within and against various theological viewpoints. At the same time, neither text is theologically rigorous or consistent, or in full accord with any particular theologian. As distinct products of the English Reformation—a series of reformations in which various theologies were appropriated piecemeal rather than as unified wholes—neither play is theologically pure or precise. Indeed, the reformational *King Leir* seems at times to endorse certain traditional practices such as praying upon "beades" and going on "pilgrimage" (perhaps in keeping with the setting of the play in the remote Christian past), while Shakespeare's *Lear* at times suggests theological values that radically out-reform the reformational *Leir*. Yet as a general pattern, the source play *Leir* tends to uphold more reformational and Calvinistic values and assumptions, while Shakespeare's revisionary *Lear* tends to undermine and repudiate such assumptions. In effect, the two stage plays offer conflicting and competing interpretations of English reformational Christianity.[2]

Before turning to the two plays, however, we need to survey the theological developments and controversies in early modern England, the contexts out of which both texts emerged. As revisionist historians have argued, the Reformation in England was rarely a unified movement in which reformed doctrines were steadily and progressively appropriated into English culture. On the contrary, England underwent a series of reformations that were contested and resisted at every stage. Virtually all historical evidence indicates that Henry's political reformation was not embraced by a populace discontent with ecclesiastical corruption. Instead, Henry's reforms were forced by government dictate upon a stubborn and resistant population—a process of coercion rather than conversion (Haigh, *Reformations* 21; Duffy 379–423). On the eve of Henry's reformation, the Church in England was a relatively healthy and robust institution that satisfied popular spiritual and cultural needs. Religious guilds and fraternities thrived, tithe disputes were relatively infrequent, and official complaints against corrupt clergy were remarkably rare (see Scarisbrick 19–39; Haigh, *Reformations* 35, 42–47). While in Germany popular discontent was expressed by rioting iconoclasts, in England altars and images were carefully removed in response to government orders—and often hid away and kept safe in expectation of future need (Haigh, *Reformations* 13). Sixteenth-century English wills (which survive in large numbers representing virtually all social classes) testify to high levels of popular satisfaction with the Church. Indeed, in the early sixteenth century all but a tiny percent of wills (perhaps three or four percent) left something for the Church; contributions declined dramatically only after the Reformation began (Scarisbrick 2–18, 187–88). Likewise, church building and rebuilding projects thrived in the early century, but then dropped to extremely low levels for the rest of the century (Scarisbrick 13–14). Similarly, endowments for masses fell into significant decline only after Henry began to seize church properties—at which point mass endowments most likely seemed a bad investment (Haigh, *Reformations* 70). Moreover, Henry's suppression of the monasteries was strongly resisted, and by protestors whose primary concerns were not political or economic but religious.[3] Even Henry, late in his reign, stepped back from the reformation by persecuting reformers and restoring elements of the old faith in the Six Articles of 1539 (see Cressy and Ferrell 3).

The more doctrinal reforms of Edward likewise met widespread resistance: contributions to parish churches declined dramatically and recruitment to the priesthood almost ceased (Haigh, *Reformations* 181–82). Mary's counter-reformational reign, though traditionally seen by historians as a mere aberration or a temporary setback, seems to have been greeted with considerable popular approval. Churchwardens' accounts indicate that the reconstruction of Catholic altars—though far more costly than Edwardian deconstruction—proceeded quickly, sometimes in advance of official orders.[4]

The subsequent Elizabethan settlement, though celebrated by many Elizabethans such as Richard Hooker, seems to have settled very little. Reforms, even moderate and ambiguous reforms, continued to face stubborn resistance. The Act for Uniformity (1559) was passed by a margin of only three votes—and only after Elizabeth imprisoned Catholic bishops and pressured or bought off nobles (Haigh, *Reformations* 241). The Elizabethan regime attempted to maximize popular approval by striking a conciliatory balance, retaining a basically Catholic style of liturgy while moving toward a more Calvinist doctrine. Yet substantial concessions were made to accommodate traditional beliefs and practices. The 1599 version of the Book of Common Prayer eliminated denunciations of the Pope, omitted the Edwardian "Black Rubric" (which denied "any real and essential presence" in the communion bread), adjusted the language for administering communion to allow for a more Catholic interpretation, and restored the wearing of the cope by the priest during communion (see Duffy 567; Cressy and Ferrell 47–48).

With similar conciliatory effects, the Thirty-nine Articles (1563) standardized Elizabethan doctrine in terms succinct and vague enough to accommodate a wide spectrum of theological interpretations.[5] Moreover, the traditional style of the English liturgy was sometimes exploited by priests who would omit parts of the Prayer Book, add Latin prayers, or even say a Catholic mass in private and then distribute consecrated hosts in a reformed service (Haigh, *Reformations* 248). Lay people would sometimes resist reforms by attending English services with Catholic beads and Latin primers in hand, or they would stand while the Gospel was read, or kneel at the name of Jesus, or refuse to receive communion in their hands but only accept it in their mouths (Duffy 577–79). Even though episcopal visitations under Elizabeth could be especially thorough and rigorous (having learned their lesson from the ineffective visitations under Edward), compliance was often reluctant and delayed. Churchwardens' accounts indicate that about half of English parishes kept their vestments and mass utensils (often hidden in private houses) for at least a full decade into Elizabeth's reign (Haigh, *Reformations* 247; Duffy 573–75).

By the 1580s, however, as the settlement seemed more settled, as the generation of Marian priests (ordained as Catholics) began to die off, and as an excommunicated Elizabeth faced the threat of a Spanish invasion, overt Catholicism became less tolerated and more often construed as political nonconformity. A 1585 statute made it treason for a Catholic priest ordained abroad to enter England, as well as treason for anyone to offer aid or shelter. Yet even though Catholicism became a persecuted religion, court records indicate that the number of recusancy cases rose dramatically, and continued to rise until the beginning of the seventeenth century.[6] Such a rise primarily reflects increased vigilance on the part of government and local officials, but also suggests the continuing appeal of the old religion (although recusants may have refused to attend English services for a variety of reasons, including apathy, laziness, or even fear of debt collectors who customarily waited outside of church).[7] Evidence of both change and resistance to change can also be seen in the preambles of wills, which in the course of the sixteenth century tended to shift, not from Catholic to Protestant versions, but from Catholic to more neutral and politically correct versions. Even late in the century, distinctly Protestant preambles appear only in a small minority of wills (Haigh, *Reformations* 200; Duffy 507–8).[8]

By the end of Elizabeth's reign, practicing Catholicism became more and more limited to the households of noble and gentry landowners. Yet the religious conformity of the majority did not signal the demise of traditional religion and the final triumph of reform; instead, much of traditional religion was absorbed and appropriated into the reformed Church. Indeed, the reformational Prayer Book itself often became a mainstay of traditional beliefs and practices, a site of resistance against the demands of radical reformers (Duffy 588–91). As virtually all reformers agreed, the majority of English people had not been reformed, at least not reformed enough.

King James, while he generally sustained the Elizabethan settlement, at times moved in a decidedly anti-reformational direction. At the Hampton Court Conference in 1604, for example, James rejected every petition put forward by the Puritans, except for their request for a new translation of the Bible. Moreover, the Canons of 1604 upheld the practices of kneeling in church, using the sign of the cross in baptism, and wearing traditional apparel by archbishops and bishops. In 1605, Archbishop Bancroft almost certainly overstated the case when he complained that "so many priests and jesuits range about in our dioceses." Yet even if practicing Catholics were a very small minority, residual Catholicism continued as a powerful force in English society.[9]

My argument is not that Shakespeare was a closet Catholic, but that traditional theological values and assumptions strongly persisted in Shakespeare and in his audiences. While the source *Leir* emerges from and appeals to the more reformational tendencies in Elizabethan culture (perhaps appealing especially to the nationalistic Protestant fervor of 1588), Shakespeare's *Lear* (written in the unreformational reign of James I) appeals to the widespread and persistent distrust of reformed theologies. While the old *Leir* implicitly and subtextually celebrates the reformational and Calvinistic values of grace, the absolute sovereignty of God's will, and the certainty of redemption for the elect, Shakespeare's revisionary *Lear* endorses the values of human works and purgatorial suffering, and dramatizes an arduous struggle toward an uncertain and indeterminate redemption. In rewriting *Leir*, Shakespeare does not merely borrow hints of plot and character, but refutes and counters the source text—in effect, Shakespeare writes an anti-*Leir* play.[10]

The reformational tendencies in the anonymous *King Leir* are often not precisely Calvinist but rather Calvinistic—reductive derivations from Calvin's theology. Calvin, for example, does not attribute absolute or perfect virtue to the elect. Following St. Paul, Calvin argues that the elect are sinners, condemned by the high standards of the Law but saved by a freely given grace. Yet, according to Calvin, the gift of grace inspires the elect to strive for the pure integrity and righteousness demanded by the Law: "The whole life of Christians ought to be a sort of practice of godliness, for we have been called to sanctification. Here it is the function of the law, by warning men of their duty, to arouse them to a zeal for holiness and innocence" (*Institutes* 3.19.2; also see 1.2.1–2). Thus, Calvin does indirectly associate election with a saintly and pious life. This association, however, became far more strong in popular conceptions (or misconceptions) of Calvin. Indeed, it is this popular notion of Calvinistic godliness that seems so prominent in the anonymous *King Leir*.

Perhaps the most distinctive feature of *Leir*, in opposition to *Lear*, is in the extreme piety and virtue of the king. With the exception of his rash response to Cordella during the love test, the Leir of the old play is not once depicted out of temper. At no point in the play do we have cause to doubt his claim to a life of habitual purity and innocence:

For her except, whom I confesse I wrongd,
Through doting frenzy, and o're-jelous love.
There lives not any under heavens bright eye,
That can convict me of impiety. (376)

From the opening scene, Leir is depicted as a king of immense, almost un-
wavering piety. He commends his recently deceased wife for her "perfit
patterne of a vertuous life" (337), and he humbly submits himself to the
will of God: "Herein, my Lords, your wishes sort with mine, / And mine (I
hope) do sort with heavenly powers" (338). His motives for resigning his
throne are most assuredly devout and even saintly: "I would fayne resigne
these earthly cares, / And thinke upon the welfare of my soule," "And here I
do freely dispossesse my selfe . . . And take me to my prayers and my
beades" (337, 350).

Moreover, the virtuous Leir insists upon dividing his kingdom into equal
shares. Against the advice of Skalliger (counterpart to Oswald), the king refuses to offer his daughters unequal dowries:

No more, nor lesse, but even all alike,
My zeal is fixt, all fashioned in one mould:
Wherefore unpartiall shall my censure be,
Both old and young shall have alike for me. (338)

Thus, the saintly Leir in no way provokes or intensifies daughterly rivalry.
Instead, Skalliger manipulates and deceives Gonorill and Ragan by misre-
porting the king's plans:

And looke, whose answere pleaseth him the best,
They shall have most unto their marriages. (341)

The supremely innocent and pious king seems, like his deceased wife, one of
the elect—a man possessed with Calvinistic grace.

Even Leir's misbegotten plan to arrange a love test springs from the most
benign motives. He arranges the test as part of a roundabout strategy to ensure a future of "perfit peace" (338) by securing marriages for all three
daughters. While Gonorill and Ragan are willing to marry Cornwall and
Cambria, his youngest daughter has found no monarch to her liking and refuses to marry "unlesse love allowes" (338). The king devises the love test in
expectation that Cordella will profess her love, and then he will be able to
manipulate her into marriage:

> . . . when they joyntly shall contend,
> Eche to exceed the other in their love:
> Then at the vantage will I take Cordella,
> Even as she doth protest she loves me best,
> Ile say, Then, daughter, graunt me one request,
> To shew thou lovest me as thy sisters doe,
> Accept a husband, whom myself will woo. . . .
> Then will I tryumph in my policy,
> And match her with a King of Brittany. (339)

Of course, the scheme fails miserably. Cordella refuses to "paynt [her] duty forth in words" (344), and in a fit of rashness Leir disowns her. Yet the strategic miscalculations of Leir are presented in the play not as manifestations of deep-rooted folly, but as isolated lapses of judgment in an otherwise virtuous king.

Even after suffering indignities at the hands of Gonorill—who cuts his allowance in half and then eliminates it altogether—the king endures all with steadfast piety and humility. As Perillus (counterpart to Kent) aptly remarks, "But he, the myrrour of mild patience, / Puts up all wrongs, and never gives reply" (355). Though Gonorill accuses the king of acting "always in extremes" and of instigating "discord and disgrace" (342, 358), we never see any evidence of such rashness. Instead, we see Gonorill fabricating lies:

> Well, after him Ile send such thunderclaps
> Of slaunder, scandall, and invented tales
> That all the blame shall be remov'd from me,
> And unperceiv'd rebound upon himselfe. (361)

Though confronted with ungrateful daughters, the saintly and long-suffering Leir assumes all guilt upon his own head and even insists upon the justice of his own suffering:

> This punishment my heavy sinnes deserve,
> And more then this ten thousand thousand times:
> Else aged Leir them could never find
> Cruell to him, to whom he hath bin kind. (358)

He is quick to realize the errors of his ways—or rather his single error in disinheriting Cordella.

In reworking the source text, Shakespeare rejects not only the Christian context of the play but the Calvinistic piety of the king. Shakespeare compounds the single error of Leir into an array of degraded vices in Lear—a king of immense pride and habitual impatience, a king for whom the malicious slanders of Gonoril are not mere fabrications. For Shakespeare's king, the love test serves no particular marital or political purpose. Instead, Lear exploits the love test as a spectacle of vanity, an attempt to coerce public adoration. While the Leir of the old play refuses unequal dowries, Shakespeare's Lear arranges a contest for larger shares (even though, ironically, he has already divided the map, apparently with the god-like presumption that he can predetermine the responses of his daughters). The absence of any adequate or stated purpose for the love test suggests a range of hidden, unspoken, "darker purposes" (1.34) on the part of the king—not merely a craving for flattery, but a desire for absolute mastery over his daughters, a longing to be the godlike focal point of all love and adoration, perhaps even a quasi-incestuous ambition to displace his daughters' husbands.

Yet Shakespeare does not entirely dismiss the *Leir* version of the love test, but develops and expands upon suggestions already present in the source text. A less benign motive for the love test in *Leir* is briefly suggested when the king remarks that he will "try which of my daughters loves me best: / Which till I know, I cannot be in rest" (339). Moments later, Skalliger maliciously exaggerates the king's concerns, describing Leir as an obsessive and doting fool:

> He earnestly desireth for to know,
> Which of you three do beare most love to him,
> And on your loves he so extremely dotes,
> As ever any did, I think, before.
> He presently doth meane to send for you,
> To be resolv'd of this tormenting doubt. (341)

Though the primary motives of Leir are clearly benign, nevertheless the old play provides various complications and even contradictions that Shakespeare seems to seize upon and exploit.

Unlike the prayerful and retiring Leir, Shakespeare's king tyrannically attempts to maintain all power—even in the very act of giving it away. Instead of submitting to the will of the gods, Lear habitually assumes command over them: "For by the sacred radiance of the sun," "Now, by Apollo," "All the stored vengeances of heaven fall / On her ingrateful top!" (1.102, 1.151, 7.320–21). Likewise Lear assumes command over the forces of nature, ordering "lightnings" to blind Regan's eyes, and "fen-sucked fogs" to blast her pride (7.323–26). While the king in the old play retains not even a single servant, Shakespeare's king attempts to retain all the privileges and perks of royalty, while free from all cares and burdens. Moreover, Lear's casting off of his kingly responsibilities appears distinctly premature—and thus even less legitimate. In contrast to Leir whose "dotage" is emphasized repeatedly (341, 356, 365, 376, 392), Shakespeare's king appears remarkably robust—hunting, feasting, refusing to "stay a jot for dinner" (4.7). While Leir retires to his prayers and beads, Lear's primary (though unspoken) desire to relinquish the throne seems entirely worldly and hedonistic.

While Leir speaks a language of Christian piety, Shakespeare's Lear speaks a language of pagan philosophic materialism. Contrary to the Christian or Thomistic view of creation *ex nihilo* (Aquinas, ch. 69), Lear insists that "Nothing can come of nothing" (1.82)—implicitly upholding the atomistic philosophy of Lucretius: "And this is the first of Nature's basic principles: / no thing can ever be produced by the gods from nothing" (5). Shakespeare's pre-Christian play, however, does not jettison Christianity, but rather displaces Christianity from the king to the figure of France. In direct opposition to Lear, France evokes the anti-pagan, anti-materialist theology of St. Paul:

> Love is not love
> When it is mingled with respects that stands
> Aloof from the entire point.
>> (1.230–32, compare 1 Corinthians 13:4–7)

> Fairest Cordelia, that art most rich, being poor;
> Most choice, forsaken; and most loved, despised.
>> (1.241–42, compare 2 Corinthians 6:10)

In effect, Lear's coercive ideology of power and landed wealth is posed against France's counter-ideology of miracle and paradox. For France, something can indeed come of nothing: "Gods, gods! 'Tis strange that from their cold'st neglect / My love should kindle to inflamed respect" (1.245–46). In violation of Lear's rational economy of exchanges (flattery for land), France's affection for Cordelia is miraculously and quite irrationally increased after she is reduced to "little seeming substance" and "nothing else" (1.188–90).[11]

While in *Leir* the Gallian King is not even present during the love test (but instead arrives several scenes later to woo Cordella), in *Lear* France becomes a major player from the start, and expounds upon Christian mysteries far more substantial and complex than the symbolic Christian attire of his counterpart (who disguises himself in "Palmers weeds" [346]). Ironically, in terms of developed theology, Shakespeare's pre-Christian France seems far more Christian than the explicitly Christian Gallian King. Moreover, the Christianity of Shakespeare's France is reflected and compounded in the figure of Kent, whose service and self-sacrifice well exceed the virtues of his counterpart Perillus in the old play. Though Perillus is briefly threatened by Leir, he is never banished, but rather embraced by the king as a faithful friend and companion throughout the play. Kent, in contrast, is despised and rejected; yet Kent returns as Caius to serve a considerably less deserving king. Like France's love for Cordelia, Kent's service to Lear is a miracle of love unrewarded and freely given—another instance in which indeed something comes of nothing. Shakespeare further compounds the theme of unrewarded and sacrificial love in the figures of Gloucester (who is blinded for his efforts to protect the king), Edgar (who returns to aide his unworthy father), and Cornwall's servant (who dies attempting to save Gloucester). In opposition to the easy and requited virtues of the old play, Shakespeare radicalizes Christian virtues in his revisionary play, re-presenting Christianity not in terms of a static and passive faith but in terms of work, struggle, and sacrifice.

In *Leir*, the king returns to a state of grace almost instantly—or rather he never quite steps out of grace. After suffering abuse from Gonorill, Leir quickly repents for his mistake in disinheriting Cordella: "Oh, how thy words adde sorrow to my soule, / To thinke of my unkindnesse to Cordella! / Whom causelesse I did dispossesse of all" (359). Yet Leir's recognition of his youngest daughter's virtue constitutes almost the entirety of his reformational process in the play. He continues to suffer, but his suffering is limited in scope and duration. Aside from two brief flirtations with despair, his torments never exceed the physical hardships of fatigue and hunger. Even when confronted by the assassin sent by Ragan to kill Leir and Perillus in a "thicket" (370), the king's fears are quickly alleviated by a timely stroke of divine intervention. Threatened by the assassin, Perillus calls to the heavens for protection and justice:

> Oh just Jehova, whose almighty power
> Doth governe all things in this spacious world,
> How canst thou suffer such outragious acts
> To be committed without just revenge? (377)

As the stage instructions indicate, the heavens are quick to respond: *"It thunders. He quakes, and lets fall the Dagger next to Perillus"* (379). Perillus then aptly remarks, "Oh, happy sight! he meanes to save my Lord. / The King of heaven continue this good mind" (379–380). As a pious and saintly king, Leir seems at all times to enjoy the special care and favor of Providence. (I would also add that the providential thunder that saves Leir from the assassin may evoke an association with the widely celebrated storm which saved Reformation England from the Catholic Spanish Armada, especially since the *Leir* play was most likely written and performed shortly after 1588.)

Though claims of providential intervention were commonplace in all Christian traditions, the constant attentiveness and intimacy of a sovereign God—"whose almighty power / Doth governe all things in this spacious world"—seems distinctly reformational and Calvinistic. Consistently in *King Leir*, apparent accidents and chance occurrences are interpreted by characters as expressions of a controlling and ever-attentive Providence. Cordella, for instance, interprets her chance meeting with the Gallian King as a sign of providential designs: "My kingly husband. . . By [God's] appointment was ordayned for me" (363). Later in the play, Leir reassures the exhausted Perillus by saying, "let us go, and see what God will send; / When all meanes faile, he is the surest friend" (388), and, indeed, in the very next scene the two men are rescued by Cordella and the Gallian King—and again Perillus aptly responds, "The blessed God of heaven hath thought upon us" (390). Like many reformers, Calvin gave special emphasis to God's absolute control over the world and intimacy in all human affairs, especially the affairs of the elect. While Thomas Aquinas gave allowances for the effects of contingency and chance (on the level of secondary causes), Calvin left virtually nothing to chance, denounced all such explanations as pagan, and insisted on God's absolute control over the world: "God's providence, as it is told in Scripture, is opposed to fortune and fortuitous happenings," "anyone who has been taught by Christ's lips that all the hairs of his head are numbered will look farther afield for a cause, and will consider that all events are governed by God's secret plan," "By setting forth examples of this sort, the prophet shows that what are thought to be chance occurrences are just so many proofs of heavenly providence" (*Institutes* 1.16.2, 1.5.8).[12] In the *Leir* play, Cordella speaks in Calvinistic terms when she accepts her disinheritance as neither fortune nor chance but God's sovereign will: "But why accuse I fortune and my father? / No, no, it is the pleasure of my God: / And I do willingly imbrace the rod" (352).

Though Leir continues to suffer (mildly) in the play, he continues to enjoy the special favor and attentiveness of God, and is quickly restored to a full state of Calvinistic grace. Consequently, the king changes in no discernable way, but rather is restored to his former condition. Indeed, the old play emphasizes not transformation but restoration—"as earst I was before"—a phrase repeated three times (369, 374, 391). Leir begins pious and humble, and ends where he began—pious and humble. In the reformational spirit of the old *Leir*, grace involves neither work nor struggle—it is absolute and is freely given.[13]

Like Leir, Shakespeare's king also begins to suffer at the hands of Gonoril, and likewise he is quick to recognize his error in disinheriting his youngest daughter:

> O most small fault,
> How ugly didst thou in Cordelia show. . . .
> Beat at this gate that let thy folly in
> And thy dear judgement out. (4.260–66)

Yet the error for which Lear repents is merely a single manifestation of a majesty fallen to folly. Though he is a man more sinned against than sinning, Lear is a man of considerable sin—and thus his suffering is both intensified and prolonged. In opposition to the Calvinistic grace in the source play, Shakespeare's play implicitly upholds the tradition of purgatorial suffering, a process of prolonged, therapeutic suffering that does not simply restore the king to his former self but moves him towards a transformation of self. While the suffering of the old Leir merely confirms his preexistent virtue, Lear's suffering reforms and recreates his nature.

C. L. Barber argues that *King Lear* is not Christian but "post-Christian" in that the play appropriates values at the heart of traditional Christianity, but on a more restricted human level, without reference to the Christian God or the direct support of the supernatural (*The Whole Journey* 295). Yet in relation to *Leir* (in which references to the Christian God abound and the support of the supernatural is both explicit and implicit), Shakespeare's play seems to uphold and endorse values that are more substantively and more rigorously Christian. I would argue that Shakespeare's *Lear* is not post-Christian but rather post-reformational or post-Calvinistic. Shakespeare refashions the king from a man possessed with overwhelming grace to a man in whom the struggle for salvation is an arduous and ongoing process. In contrast to Leir, who briefly lapses into sin but soon recovers his saintliness, Shakespeare's king is too far gone for a Calvinistic quick fix. He endures prolonged purgatorial suffering toward a more traditional and unpredetermined redemption.

While the thunder of the old play serves as a well-timed surgical strike upon the would-be assassin, Shakespeare's storm has no effect upon Oswald or Gonoril or Regan or Edmund. Yet the raging storm in Shakespeare's play ultimately seems not a rejection but an appropriation of the providential thunder of the old play. When Shakespeare's king intertextually echoes Perillus by calling upon the heavens to punish all caitiffs and enemies of the gods, the heavens respond by beating down upon the head of one enemy of the gods—the king himself. Though the heavens ignore Lear's plea for the immediate destruction of the world, and ignore (at least temporarily) his demand for vengeance on his ungrateful daughters, his prayers are ironically answered. In effect, the guilty assassin of the source play is displaced by the king himself who becomes the object of divine wrath. Moreover, the wrath of the gods eventually turns from punitive to therapeutic—a rough justice which Lear himself comes to acknowledge and embrace:

> Expose thyself to feel what wretches feel,
> That thou mayst shake the superflux to them
> And show the heavens more just. (11.31–33)

In the intensified and prolonged torment of Shakespeare's storm, Lear begins to experience the miracles and paradoxes voiced by France. Indeed, once again something (compassion and fellow-feeling) comes of nothing (suffering and deprivation):

> Come on, my boy. How dost, my boy? Art cold?
> I am cold myself.—Where is this straw, my fellow?
> The art of our necessities is strange,
> That can make vile things precious. Come, your hovel.—
> Poor fool and knave, I have one part of my heart
> That sorrows yet for thee. (9.69–74)

While the king of the old play is swindled out of his royal garb by mariners in exchange for sea passage to France, Shakespeare's penitent king willingly sheds his royal garb and begins to seek the lowest and most dejected state in nature—the nakedness of Edgar. In the purgatorial storm, Lear endures a disintegration of his old self and a reduction to nothingness, from which he emerges with a new sense of humility and compassion. In the revisionary *Lear*, the chaotic storm proves unchaotic after all.

The therapeutic suffering of Lear can be more fully discerned in light of what does not happen in the old play. In *Leir*, the compassion and fellow feeling of the king are narrowly circumscribed. While traveling from Gonorill to Ragan, the exhausted king and the faithful Perillus bond in intimate fellowship:

> *Per.* Rest on me, my Lord, and stay your selfe,
> The way seemes tedious to your aged lymmes.
>
> *Leir.* Nay, rest on me, kind friend, and stay thy selfe,
> Thou art as old as I, but more kind.
>
> *Per.* Ah, good my Lord, it ill befits, that I
> Should leane upon the person of a King. . . .

> *Leir.* Cease, good Perillus, for to call me Lord,
>   And think me but the shaddow of my selfe. (364)

Under duress, the king of the old play comes to realize the common humanity he shares with his friend. Leir's humility, however, is nothing new in the
play, and his sense of fellow feeling, though perhaps intensified, remains entirely limited to Perillus.

In refashioning *Leir* into *Lear*, Shakespeare does not simply write against
the textual grain of the old play, but at times seizes upon suggestions already
present in the source text. For instance, Shakespeare does not reject but
rather intensifies and even radicalizes the fellow feelings of Leir. The compassion of Shakespeare's king extends not merely to Kent—"Prithee, go in
thyself. Seek thy own ease" (11.22)—but to the Fool, the mad Edgar, and,
above all, the infinitude of poor and suffering:

> Poor naked wretches, wheresoe'er you are,
> That bide the pelting of this pitiless night,
> How shall your houseless heads and unfed sides,
> Your looped and windowed raggedness, defend you
> From seasons such as these? O, I have ta'en
> Too little care of this. (11.25–30)

Lear's speech both intertextually evokes and radically surpasses the circumscribed and underdeveloped sympathies of the king in the source text.
Moreover, Lear's compassion emerges not in a "thicket" but in the totally
barren waste of the heath ("For many miles about / There's not a bush"
[7.458–59])—a setting in which ceremony, ritual, courtly garb, and hierarchy are more thoroughly negated. In the social leveling and radical minimalism of the barren heath, Shakespeare's play not only counter-reforms but
out-reforms the reformational tendencies of the source text.[14]

In the old play, reformational values are particularly emphasized when
the king, while out in the "thicket," begins to pray and read "with pure zeale"
upon his book (373), most likely a Bible or devotional book. Though reading
was by no means an exclusively reformational practice, it was a distinctly
reformational and Protestant practice.[15] Leir's reading of a Bible or religious
book on stage implies a piety not of works but of the word. On the barren
heath, Shakespeare excludes the book, and yet the absence of the book (ne-
cessitated by the pre-Christian setting) may also contribute to the more radical reformational suggestions in Shakespeare's play. The absolute
minimalism of Shakespeare's barren heath (without ceremony or courtly
garb or books) may even suggest the bare-bones simplicity of Calvin-

ism—four bare walls and a sermon, but without the walls and without the sermon. In Shakespeare's storm, we see Calvinistic minimalism appropriated and pushed to the very limits.

While in the old play Leir fully possesses the absolute truth of the book, the condition of Shakespeare's Lear remains unsteady and enigmatic. In opposition to Leir's complete sanctification by grace, Lear's purgatorial progress towards grace is slow, incremental, and often recidivistic. He calls upon the gods to give him "patience," and within the very same speech cries out for "revenges" that will be the "terrors of the earth" (7.430–41). He insists he will be "the pattern of all patience" (9.37), only to lose all patience. He feels compassion for Edgar, but can only perceive Edgar's suffering in terms of his own mistreatment by daughters.

Scholars who argue that Shakespeare's play repudiates a Christian worldview often cite such inconsistencies in the king. Jonathan Dollimore, for example, comments that "Lear experiences pity mainly as an inseparable aspect of his own grief," "Lear hardly communicates with anyone, especially on the heath," and "his preoccupation with vengeance ultimately displaces his transitory pity" (192–93). Yet such comments imply that in order to sustain a Christian vision, Shakespeare's play must follow a swift, upward trajectory toward grace and redemption—a "perfect pattern" such as that urged in Sidney's *Defence of Poetry* and fully realized in the old play (119). I would agree that Shakespeare certainly subverts such patterns, but I would argue that Shakespeare nevertheless accords with more traditional and counter-reformational Christian theologies which see redemption not as a quick fix but as the end of an arduous process of struggle and tentative advances.[16] While in the old play the king lapses into sin and is quickly restored to a full state of grace, Lear (like Gloucester) lapses and then relapses again. His failure to turn from sinner to saint does not negate Christianity, though it powerfully negates the reductive Christianity of *King Leir*.

The old play appropriates into reformational style the medieval morality pattern of sin-suffering-redemption, with redemption fully and securely achieved in the king's reunion with his faithful and faith-filled daughter. Like her father, Cordella is exceedingly pious and saintly—only more so. As Perillus describes her, "the perfit good indeed, / Can never be corrupted by the bad" (387). When disinherited in the opening scenes, she piously vows penitence and prayer to regain her father's love:

> Barefoote I would on pilgrimage set forth
> Unto the furthest quarters of the earth,
> And all my life time would I sackcloth weare,
> And mourning-wise powre dust upon my head:

> So he but to forgive me once would please,
> That his grey haires might go to heaven in peace. . . .
> I will to Church, and pray unto my Saviour,
> That ere I dye, I may obtayne his favour. (363–64)

Yet Cordella, though exceedingly devout, is remarkably inactive—more an embodiment of passive faith than active works (even though her piety is expressed partly in terms of the tradition of pilgrimage). She does not venture to England to rescue her father, but merely happens upon him while on a country walk—an accident that heaven provides, but apparently a reformational heaven that depends little on human efforts. As one of the elect—with "grace from God on hye" (380)—her virtue is innate and repeatedly expressed in her God-given symbolic beauty: "She hath a little beauty extraordinary," "God give her joy of her surpassing beauty," "she doth surpasse us both in beauty," "A fayrer creature ne're mine eyes beheld" (348, 349, 352). In keeping with the old play's emphasis on outward symbolism, Cordella rescues her father not from an inward tempest of the mind but from bodily starvation: "the gripe of famine" (390). She offers Leir a basket of food with allegorical implications he is quick to recognize:

> Me thinks, I never ate such savory meat:
> It is as pleasant as the blessed Manna,
> That raynd from heaven amongst the Israelites:
> It hath recall'd my spirits home agayne,
> And made me fresh, as earst I was before. (391)

After an elaborate ritual of kneelings (Leir kneels three times, Cordella twice), father and daughter are finally reconciled. Yet the change in Leir since the beginning of the play seems negligible. His ordeal of suffering confirms but does not develop or increase his constant piety. His return to his former condition—"as earst I was before"—is made symbolically complete by his military victory and repossession of the throne he held in the opening of the play (though ultimately he relinquishes his earthly throne to the Gallian King).

In rewriting the source text, Shakespeare refashions the outward "Palmers weeds" of the Gallian King into the inward Pauline theology of France and the passive beauty of Cordella into the active virtues of Cordelia (who seeks out and rescues her father). Moreover, Shakespeare describes the pre-Christian Cordelia in a series of highly suggestive Christian images:

> There she shook
> The holy water from her heavenly eyes. (17.30–31)

> O dear father,
> It is thy business that I go about. (18.24–25)

> Thou hast one daughter
> Who redeems nature from the general curse
> Which twain hath brought her to. (20.194–96)[17]

Such images both evoke and exceed the saintliness of Cordella in the old play in that Shakespeare's heroine expresses both the virtues of reformational faith and the virtues of counter-reformational works. While her counterpart (out on a country stroll) enjoys a providentially arranged reunion with her father, Cordelia raises an army to go about her father's business, takes active measures to redeem nature. In Shakespeare's revisionary play the patterns of medieval morality plays are more fully activated, with the role of Good Deeds restored in the figure of Cordelia (and compounded in Kent, Gloucester, Edgar, and Cornwall's servant). In the old play Good Deeds is conspicuously absent; thus the forces of goodness and justice always descend from above in the form of an interventionist, Calvinistic God. In *Lear* the forces of goodness rise from below in active works and human efforts.

As Cordelia's virtue is more active and inward, so is Lear's transformation of character. While the king of the old play suffers primarily from outward physical hardships, the suffering of Shakespeare's king is radically internalized. In the old play, the king's most extreme suffering is in the form of hunger, a point belabored throughout the reconciliation scene: "I do faint for want of sustenance," "How neere they are to death for want of food," "Vouchsafe to save us from the gripe of famine" (389–90). Shakespeare's Lear, on the contrary, endures an inward "rage," a "tempest in the mind," in which he is "cut to the brains" (21.76, 11.12, 20.181). In the intensity of Lear's psychic turmoil, physical hardships become merely incidental, indeed are "scarce felt" (11.9)—perhaps an intertextual dig at the mild ordeals of the king in the old play. Further, while the old play insists upon Leir's condition as one of "great extremity," "this extremity," "such extremity" (386, 387, 388), Shakespeare makes the king's condition extreme indeed.

Instead of a "blessed banquet," Shakespeare's Lear is revived by sleep and music—nourishment for the mind and inward spirit.[18] Salvaged from madness, he is spiritually reborn: "child-changed," in "fresh garments," baptized into innocence by the "holy water" from Cordelia's eyes (21.15, 20, 17.31). Purged of his colossal vanity, he awakens with a new-found patience and humility—"Pray now, forget and forgive. I am old / And foolish" (21.83–84)—a simplicity of words that marks not a return to his former self but a hard-earned recreation of self.

In Shakespeare's reconciliation scene Cordelia refuses her father's attempt to kneel, a refusal that suggests an intertextual repudiation of the outwardness of the old play. As on the barren heath, Shakespeare deritualizes the scene, rejecting ceremony and symbolism in favor of profound inwardness, intimacy, and silence—a bare-bones, minimalist Christianity that out-reforms the source (and perhaps out-Calvins Calvin).

Lear's dynamic transformation, as opposed to Leir's static restoration, can also be gauged by the company he keeps. While the pious Leir spends most of the play in the faithful company of the pious Perillus, Shakespeare's king advances through multiple phases of companionship, starting with the worldly and pragmatic wisdom of the Fool, advancing to Prophetic and Old Testament wisdom of Edgar, and culminating in the charity and New Testament wisdom of Cordelia. While in the old play the king gains nothing from Perillus that he does not already possess in his heart or in his book, in Shakespeare's play the king suffers into wisdom by means of intermediaries—in ways that may suggest the traditions of priestly or saintly intercessors.

Moreover, when finally Lear is reunited with Cordelia, the Christian mystery of something coming from nothing is further unfolded: Cordelia offers her father not the poison he deserves but forgiveness and charity that he does not deserve (at least according to the rationalist and materialist philosophy of Lear in the opening scene). Lear is indeed a man more sinned against than he deserves, but he is also a man more forgiven than he deserves. While the old play looks to a Deuteronomic tradition of virtue rewarded and sin punished—a reductive calculus rejected by both Thomas Aquinas and John Calvin—Shakespeare's more rigorously Christian play consistently repudiates any such precise calculus.

Many scholars acknowledge various Christian developments in *King Lear*, but conclude that such developments are ultimately and brutally subverted in the tragic ending.[19] Such interpretations, however, seem based on the assumption that the only type of ending that could sustain a Christian vision would be an ending similar to that of the old play. Yet the Christianity of the old *Leir* is what Shakespeare refutes and undermines from the very start. The consequences of virtue in Shakespeare's play are not poetic and worldly justice, but harsh and undeserved suffering. The profound sense of negation at the end of Shakespeare's play seems directed not at Christianity (at least not Christianity in its higher registers) but at the simplistic and reductive Christian pieties of the source play.

As in all earlier versions of the story (as well as Natham Tate's revision of Shakespeare's revision), the source play ends with a triumph of poetic justice as the king reunites with his faithful daughter, defeats his enemies, and reclaims the throne. When Leir and the Gallian King invade England, the intimate and ever-attentive Calvinistic God once again intervenes on Leir's behalf as the coastal watchmen, assigned to fire the "Beacon" on the approach of any invading fleet, are suddenly inspired to head off to a local tavern for ale and a "rasher of Bacon" (397). Unprepared, the town is taken with ease and a good deal of humor: the soldiers "skirmish but with naked men," while the clown Mumford "incountred with naked women" (397, 399). The power of faith and the absolute sovereignty of God's interventionist will is repeatedly emphasized in the final moments of the play as the Gallian King proclaims, "Thanks be to God, your foes are overcome," and King Leir responds, "First to the heavens, next, thanks to you, my sonne," to which the Gallian King then responds, "Thank heavens, not me" (401–02). Though such remarks are common in all Christian traditions (as well as in Shakespeare's history plays), the heavy-handed and belabored emphasis on God's absolute sovereignty in the source play strikes a Calvinistic note. Many scholars have suggested an analogy between Shakespeare's Lear and the Biblical Job; ultimately, however, it is the Leir of the old play who most resembles Job—at least the Job who in the end enjoys the redoubled blessings of a just and intervening God.

In rewriting *Leir* as *Lear*, Shakespeare repeatedly seems to elicit expectations for a similar outcome of worldly and poetic justice, but only to undermine and brutally sabotage such expectations. Edgar, particularly, seems an intertextual voice evoking the dependable and even-handed justice of the old play. In a line that could serve as a faithful choric commentary on *King Leir*, Edgar proclaims that "The worst returns to laughter" (15.6). In Shakespeare's play, however, we soon discover that in spite of Edgar's choric reassurances the worst does not return to laughter, but gets much worse still: with subversively precise timing Gloucester enters the stage with bleeding eyes. Yet while the poetic justice of the old play is savagely undermined, Edgar begins to develop a more subtle and complex sense of ultimate, providential justice. In response to the grotesque sight of his father, Edgar does not abandon faith in justice, but adapts and reconstitutes his faith: "The worst is not / As long as we can say 'This is the worst' " (15.25–26). Edgar's recuperation of faith in some deferred, ultimate justice—in the face of all evidence to the contrary—seems a key moment of departure from the source text. While in the old play the king's faith is solidly confirmed by worldly justice and providential intervention, in Shakespeare's play Edgar's faith is strained beyond all limits—and then strained further still. Yet even in the final scene of the play, Edgar (in spite of further setbacks) continues to sustain faith in providential justice: "The gods are just, and of our pleasant vices / Make instruments to scourge us" (24.166–67). Though Edgar's comment may seem formulaic or even callous, I would argue that by the end of the play Edgar's resilient faith has evolved well beyond simplistic pieties. Indeed, Edgar urges his father to "pray that the right may thrive" (23.2) while he makes careful preparations in case the right does not thrive. In his resilient faith, Edgar makes provisions for both a military victory and a military defeat—which, by means of Gonoril's letter and the challenge to Edmund, he plans to turn into a victory. The naive faith of Edgar in the earlier scenes (akin to the old play) is superseded by a more subtle and patient faith in the final scenes.[20]

Yet worldly and poetic justice is not entirely abandoned in Shakespeare's play. Though Lear and Cordelia lose the war, Gonoril, Regan, and Edmund do not win. The virtuous Albany (more virtuous than his counterpart Cambria) seizes control by exposing the villainy of his wife and rendering Edmund militarily impotent—"for thy soldiers, / All levied in my name, have in my name / Took their discharge" (24.102–04)—a strategic move that in effect makes Albany the military victor. Shakespeare even embellishes the ending with instances of poetic justice without any precedent in the source play. While in *Leir* the evil daughters maintain a unified alliance and at the end escape unharmed, in *Lear* the unholy alliance of Gonoril and Regan quickly breaks down in "likely wars" (6.10) and sexual rivalry, and in the end murder and suicide. Moreover, in an incident without precedent in *Leir* (or in the source of the subplot, Sidney's *Arcadia*), Edgar achieves a poetically just victory in a trial by combat over his bastard brother (the bastard in the *Arcadia* never confronts his brother in single combat, and survives at the end to plan further villainy).

In Shakespeare's play, poetic justice is not simply trashed, but repeatedly evoked, partially fulfilled—and then trashed. After the successful trial by combat and the other embellished instances of poetic justice, the play ends with at best a pyrrhic victory. Shakespeare heightens and intensifies our expectations for a just outcome for Cordelia, but only to undermine poetic justice once and for all in her poetically unjust execution. The final moments of the play offer a series of powerful, if not overwhelming, negations: Albany calls to the gods to defend Cordelia (while Lear enters with her dead body), Lear says that if the feather stirs all his sorrows are redeemed (but the feather does not stir), and finally Albany proclaims that all friends shall enjoy the wages of their virtue (and yet Cordelia dies while rats enjoy good health).

The profoundly unpoetic ending, however, seems as appropriate to *Lear* as poetic justice seems a fitting and necessary ending to *Leir*. The old play consistently emphasizes worldly justice, and thus ends with military victory and the king's reacquisition of his throne. Shakespeare does not merely jettison the ending of the source, but consistently counters and refutes the source text from the very beginning: Kent, Edgar, Gloucester, and Cornwall's servant are not rewarded for their virtues but threatened, cast out, tortured, killed. The death of Cordelia in the final moments of the play both repudiates the source text and completes the trajectory of Shakespeare's revisionary text—a text in which the consequences of virtue are suffering and death. While *Leir* is a play about carrying crosses, *Lear* is a play about dying on them.

The brutally subversive and unpoetic ending of *Lear*, though it powerfully undermines the pieties of *Leir*, does not undermine the more resilient faith that emerges in Edgar, nor does Shakespeare's ending violate the more complex theological perspectives on suffering that evolved in medieval and early modern Europe. John Donne, for instance, describes suffering as a providential means of exhorting men to virtue: "affliction is a treasure, and scarce any man hath enough of it. No man hath affliction enough that is not matured, and ripened by it, and made fit for God by that affliction" ("Meditation XVII" 441). Similarly, Francis Bacon sees Providence at work in human adversities: "Prosperity is the blessing of the Old Testament; Adversity is the blessing of the New, which carrieth the greater benediction and the clearer revelation of God's favour" ("Of Adversity" 57).

Keith Thomas offers a sweeping survey of similar views, by both traditional and reformed theologians, that are in full accord on the matter of suffering as either God's judgment on the guilty or God's testing and spiritual nurturing of the innocent (90–132). Though such elastic and ultimately self-confirming views may indeed have violated any sense of consistency or logic, nevertheless such views were deeply embedded in Renaissance habits of perception. We fail to adequately historicize the ending of *King Lear* when we underestimate the capacity of Renaissance men and women to accommodate the suffering of both the guilty and the innocent into highly elastic conceptions of providential designs.

At the same time, a more Deuteronomic emphasis on immediate earthly rewards was also commonplace in Renaissance culture, especially among those who enjoyed worldly prosperity, such as the merchants and shopkeepers of London—well represented in Shakespeare's audiences. Moreover, this tendency to link virtue with prosperity, though in distinct violation of John Calvin's theology, was especially strong among the followers of Calvin. Calvin himself explicitly rejected any direct link between spiritual virtue and worldly prosperity:

> For faith does not certainly promise itself either length of years or honors or riches in this life, since the Lord willed that none of these things be appointed to us. . . . Rather, the chief assurance of faith rests in the expectation of the life to come. . . . whatever earthly miseries and calamities await those whom God has embraced in his love, these cannot hinder his benevolence from being their full happiness. (3.2.28)

Nevertheless, Calvin may have encouraged an association between Christian virtue and worldly profit by rejecting chance and insisting that all things express God's sovereign will. Ironically, Shakespeare's ending might well have suited John Calvin, but would likely have brought consternation to many of his followers. The subversive ending of Shakespeare's play may be aimed at both the Calvinistic old play as well as the reductive and simplistic Calvinistic attitudes that circulated among the more prosperous citizens of London.[21]

But even within the context of the most subtle and resilient Christian views of undeserved suffering, can the abysmal and frustrating injustice of Shakespeare's ending sustain any sense of Christian redemption? We must first keep in mind that if the play moves toward redemption, it is not the absolute and certain redemption of the old play, but an incremental, unsteady, and indeterminate redemption. Vestiges of Lear's earlier self continue to resurface as he longs for an eternal paradise with his daughter in an earthly prison—perhaps not unlike his initial desire to reside in Cordelia's "kind nursery" (1.116). Moreover, Lear boasts of killing the slave that hanged Cordelia, and he may slip into despair or madness in the final moments of the play. While the old Leir briefly sins but quickly and fully regains his saintliness (and even offers forgiveness to the would-be assassin and later forgives his elder daughters [378, 389]), Shakespeare's Lear evolves from sinner to anguished and penitent man—always on the verge of relapse. Like Gloucester who is saved from despair only to fall into "ill thoughts again" (23.9), Lear continues to grope in long-suffering confusion. While the old Leir ends in a symbolic paradise, Shakespeare's Lear remains "bound / Upon a wheel of fire" (21.45)—in purgatory. From a Calvinistic view, in which redemption is all or nothing, Lear dies unredeemed—but there are other views.

Ultimately, the question of Lear's redemption depends upon the expression on his face. Unless Edgar misleads us, we know that Gloucester, torn between joy and grief, dies "smilingly" (24.196). But in the absence of detailed stage instructions, we cannot know whether Lear dies with a smile or an expression of torment and despair—whether at the moment of his death he parallels Gloucester (as he often does) or contrasts Gloucester (as he often does). Even if Shakespeare, as director, instructed the actor playing Lear to die with a smile, such an expression would not necessarily indicate a final victory of redemptive joy over despairing grief, but could signify a relapse into madness. We are left, at best, only with the possibility that Lear dies smilingly and that his smile signifies a moment of inner redemption, a moment in which he finally does "See better" (1.150), sees the awakening of Cordelia as a "soul in bliss" in a paradise that is not an earthly prison.[22]

Yet as generations of playgoers and readers can testify, the ending of *King Lear*—in spite of the capacity for traditional and reformed theologies to accommodate (or be forced to accommodate) abysmal and undeserved suffering—nevertheless pushes faith in a providential universe to the breaking point, or beyond. Like the Book of Job—before the consoling epilogue—or like the early versions of the Gospel of Mark—which end not with the appearances of Jesus but merely with the empty tomb—*King Lear* offers not consolation but a harsh and bitter confrontation with the price of virtue. The final moments of the play may convey an unbearable sense of negation, but we should consider that at least some of the force of that negation may be directed not at Christian faith in a providential universe but at pious faith in a poetically just universe. Like the play at large, the final scene may subvert not Christianity in all forms but the Christianity of the old play.

Notes

1. See, for example, Calderwood 5–19; Dollimore 189–203; and Elton. Also see the views of Jan Kott, F. Wilson, D. G. James, Robert G. Hunter, and Nicholas Brooke in G. R. Hibbard's "*King Lear*: A Retrospect, 1939–79," 1–25.

2. Many commentators have made passing remarks about the relationship between *Leir* and *Lear*, but the most detailed study is by William R. Elton (63–71). Elton concludes that Shakespeare undermines the Christianity of *Leir*, yet Elton deals with Christianity in general terms—not in the context of competing versions of Christianity in the English Reformation. For general comparisons of the play and source, see Greg 377–400; Bullough 7: 276–83; and Muir 197–201. For studies of the structural changes made by Shakespeare, see Perkinson 315–29 and Law 112–24. For a feminist approach to *Lear* and *Leir*, see McEachern 269–90. For an earlier, shorter, non-historicized version of the present chapter, see Lynch 161–74.

3. As Haigh argues, economic grievances in the Pilgrimage of Grace were distinctly of secondary importance and seem to have been added later (*Reformations* 148). I would add that though current critical and theoretical trends tend to insist that everything is ultimately political, popular resistance to the English Ref-

ormation often suggests that the most vital motivations of protestors were primarily religious, and that in many instances religion was not a disguised form of politics, but rather politics was a disguised form of religion.

4. See Haigh, *Reformations* 211, 235. Haigh comments that "Historians have often regarded Mary's reign as an aberration, an inconvenient disruption of the natural process of Reformation," yet "From the perspective of 1558 (if not of 1559), it is the reign of Edward that appears an aberration, disrupting the process of Catholic restoration which had begun in 1538 and was to continue under Mary."

5. See Cressy and Ferrell 59–70. Predestination, for example, is upheld in the Thirty-nine Articles, but only in general terms—as it is upheld by Thomas Aquinas, the Council of Trent, and Ignatius Loyola. The vagueness of the Articles was a major source of consternation for radical reformers.

6. See Williams 284–85 and Scarisbrick 137. Scarisbrick comments that recusancy was common not merely in a few isolated strongholds such as Lancashire, but in virtually all regions of England.

7. I would add that many recusants may have longed for old-time religion, not out of devout piety, but for lack of it. The reassuring rituals of the old faith (including such quasi-magical practices as blessing fields, flocks, and wells) likely seemed attractive alternatives to the demands of more zealous clergy for an inward and informed spirituality. As Keith Thomas argues, the reformed English Church attempted to eliminate superstitious practices, yet did not offer satisfactory alternatives to comfort inevitable anxieties about weather, fire, disease, plague, and so forth (58–89).

8. Interestingly, Shakespeare's father apparently left a will (discovered in 1757 but soon lost) in a distinctly Catholic style, with references to the "true Catholic faith," "last sacrament of extreme unction," and "Purgatory" (Schoenbaum 46–49). Though John Shakespeare may have died a papist, however, he may not have lived as a papist, or raised his children as such. My argument is not that Shakespeare was a papist, but that *King Lear* moves in a more traditional direction in relation to the Calvinistic *Leir*.

9. For the Hampton Court Conference, the Canons, and Bancroft, see the relevant documents in Cressy and Ferrell 123–135.

10. All references to Shakespeare's *King Lear* are from the Quarto text, *The History of King Lear*. I have based this chapter on the Quarto since it most likely represents an early version of the play, and thus would be more closely and immediately related to the primary source. While the Folio is a revision of the Quarto, the Quarto *Lear* represents more directly Shakespeare's reworking of the source *Leir*. Generally, however, I find that the differences between the Quarto and the Folio have only minor impact upon the theological implications of the play. I will address the more pertinent differences as I go along.

11. I agree with Jonathan Dollimore that *King Lear* suggests a "dominant ideology of property and power," but I depart from Dollimore in arguing for compet-

ing ideologies in the play, especially in the emergent Pauline counter-ideology of France (201).

12. For Thomas Aquinas' views of fortune, chance, and contingency, see *Compendium*, chs. 137, 139, 140.

13. The fixed and constant piety of Leir may derive from Calvin's doctrine that election is permanent and irrevocable. Though the elect, according to Calvin, may lapse into sin, election will nevertheless shine forth in a life of godliness and virtue. See *Institutes* 3.24.4–6.

14. In opposition to Catholic traditions of hierarchy and authority, Calvin emphasizes the social leveling of reformed Christianity: "we are warned how great a feeling of brotherly love ought to be among us, since by the same right of mercy and free liberality we are equally children of such a father" (*Institutes* 3.20.38).

15. See Haigh, *Reformations* 276, 287. For Calvin's emphasis on the authority and indispensability of the Bible, see *Institutes* 1.6.1–4.

16. Thomas Aquinas comments that "unyielding adherence to good or to evil pertains to the end of life's course; immobility and cessation from activity are the terminus of movement. On the other hand, the whole of our present life is a time of wayfaring, as is shown by man's changeableness both in body and in soul" (ch. 145). Likewise, the Catholic reformer Ignatius Loyola continually assumes in his *Spiritual Exercises* that Christians will experience innumerable setbacks and relapses in pursuit of personal reform.

17. The first of these three quotes was deleted in the Folio text (along with all of scene 17), but the other two passages remained. The deletion seems typical of the rather minor differences in theological emphasis between the Folio and the Quarto.

18. Although "music" (21.23) is explicitly mentioned only in the Quarto, the Folio line "untuned and jarring senses" implies music even more strongly than the Quarto line "untuned and hurrying senses" (21.14). With or without musical accompaniment, the scene certainly emphasizes an inward healing beyond the physical hunger of Leir in the source. Moreover, earlier versions of the story in Geoffrey of Monmouth's *Historia Anglicana* and Holinshed's *Second Booke of the Historie of England* depict the youngest daughter rescuing her father by sending money and servants—only in Shakespeare's version is the emphasis on an inward healing of the mind and spirit (see Bullough 7: 314, 318).

19. Calderwood, for example, comments that "The consolations of Christian philosophy are temptingly offered but cruelly withdrawn" (9); Dollimore remarks that "The timing of these two deaths [of Cordelia and Lear] must surely be seen as cruelly, precisely, subversive" (203); and Elton argues that "Lear's newfound 'faith' is pathetically and suddenly withdrawn from him by the murder of Cordelia" and that "the devastating fifth act shatters, more violently than an earlier apostasy might have done, the foundations of faith itself" (262, 337).

20. Stephen Greenblatt, in his interpretation of Edgar, comments that "the scene at Dover is a disenchanted analysis of both religious and theatrical illu-

sions," "*King Lear* is haunted by a sense of rituals and beliefs that are no longer ef-
ficacious, that have been *emptied out*"(118–19). I would argue, on the contrary,
that though Edgar's efforts to save his father from despair do not work fully that
does not mean they do not work at all. Edgar's persistent and resilient providential
faith is frustrated time and time again, especially when his father relapses into despair, but at the end Gloucester dies "smilingly" (24.196). It seems to me that what
Shakespeare undermines and empties out is not Christian faith but reductive and
naive Christian faith.

   I would also add that my interpretation of Edgar depends little on whether he
(according to the Folio) or Albany (according to the Quarto) speaks the final lines
of the play. My hunch, however, is that the Quarto attribution is a misprint, and
that in both versions Shakespeare intended Edgar to speak the closing lines (and
by implication assume rule over the kingdom). Edgar is a more fully developed
character than Albany, and the phrase "We that are young" seems more suited to
Edgar as the young brother of Edmund.

   21. For an analysis of the tendency in popular Calvinism to link prosperity
with virtue, see Thomas 102–3, 131.

   22. In the Quarto text, the possibility that the dying Lear sees anything of significance seems indeterminate in the absence of stage instructions—"O, O, O, O!"
(24.303)—though the Folio seems more suggestive—"Do you see this? Look on
her. Look, her lips. / Look there, look there" (5.3.285–86). I would also add that
Lear's death may seem not an absolute departure from the source but rather an in-
tensification of what seems suggested but underdeveloped in the source. While at
the end of *Leir* the old king relinquishes his throne to the Gallian King as a symbolic gesture of earthly transcendence, Shakespeare's king moves towards a more
radical and complete (as well as costly and sacrificial) transcendence.

CHAPTER 4

The Role of the Author in the *Confessio Amantis* and *Pericles*

In *Pericles*, Shakespeare brings the author of the source text out on stage, the only instance in all thirty-seven plays in which Shakespeare so flaunts his literary indebtedness. Though in one scene of *Titus Andronicus* (4.1), Lavinia opens the text of Ovid's *Metamorphoses* to the very tale that served as a source for the play, neither Ovid nor the *Metamorphoses* makes any further appearances. The choric Gower, however, remains a major figure throughout *Pericles*, appearing for eight choruses and speaking over three hundred lines.

Not only does Shakespeare's foregrounding of his primary source seem unusual, but his extensive use of the old-fashioned device of the chorus seems rather odd in so late a play as *Pericles*. Indeed, it is not surprising that Ben Jonson found the play a "mouldy tale," and that John Dryden mistook it for one of Shakespeare's earliest works: "Shakespeare's own Muse her Pericles first bore; / The Prince of Tyre was elder than the Moor [Aaron in *Titus Andronicus*]."[1] Perhaps Shakespeare felt compelled to resort to a choric framing device as a means of securing some measure of cohesion in dramatizing the sprawling and highly episodic narrative of Appolinus of Tyre which he found in John Gower's *Confessio Amantis* (Book VIII). Indeed, John Gower himself resorted to a type of chorus, or rather three choric voices, throughout the *Confessio*: the Confessor who instructs Amantis with moral counsel and narrates a series of exemplary moral tales, the Latin verse epigrams that serve as thematic and didactic introductions to major sections of the poem, and finally the Latin marginal glosses that serve as indices and guides to the poem. Yet unlike the various choric voices in the *Confessio*, the choric Gower in *Pericles* is not a fictive character within the story, nor an anonymous and disembodied choric voice, but a distinct author figure—he author of the primary source on which the play is based.[2]

In his late plays, Shakespeare seems particularly interested in author figures. Paulina, for example, appears in the final scene of *The Winter's Tale* as a kind of playwright and director who carefully controls and comments upon the action, while in *The Tempest* Prospero appears with book and staff (perhaps symbolic of a writer's pen) directing the various internal plays within the play. In *Pericles*, however, we have not merely an author-like figure, but an actual author figure, and an especially authorial figure if the role of the choric Gower was played by Shakespeare. Yet whether Shakespeare played the role or not, the choric-author figure of Gower almost inevitably suggests an affiliation (though not an identity) with the author of the play. At least one of Shakespeare's contemporaries seems to have fused, or confused, the roles of chorus and author: on the title page of George Wilkins' *Painfull Adventures of Pericles* (a prose version apparently based on the play) appears the description, "the true history of the play of Pericles, as it was lately presented by the worthy and ancient poet John Gower." If the choric Gower indeed suggests the author of the play, and thus serves as a surrogate for Shakespeare, what does the play suggest about Shakespeare's self-conception, after some twenty years in the theater business, of his role as an author and a playwright?[3]

Before exploring the role of the author in *Pericles*, we should consider the various and evolving conceptions of authors, and especially playwrights, in early modern England. Contrary to nineteenth-century romantic conceptions of the author as a fully autonomous and inspired genius, the role of the author in early modern England was still conceived largely in medieval terms. Like medieval cathedrals, literary texts were seen as corporate enterprises, produced not by individuals but by communities. Indeed, many medieval and Renaissance writers remained anonymous—not merely because of the losses and accidents of history, but because even in an age of emerging capitalism, authors did not assume full ownership over their texts as intellectual private property. What would it matter if we had a name to link with *Everyman* or *Edward III* or *The True Chronicle Historie of King Leir*? Such stories had earlier lineages, and were seen as products of evolving traditions more than creations of particular authors. As John Gower repeatedly reminds us in the *Confessio*, his poem is not fully authorized by him, but is a re-presentation of "olde bokes" and "cronikes" (VIII, 1160, 1554), which are themselves re-presentations of still older books and chronicles. The primary function of the author was not textual creation but textual mediation.

As faithful conveyers and transmitters of old tales to new audiences, authors might embellish, update, and modify; nevertheless, old books enjoyed more cultural authority than new authors, and new authors could only claim authority by grounding their works in old books.

In his essay, "The Death of the Author," Roland Barthes describes the author from a structuralist perspective that, ironically, may be more accurate for premodern than postmodern authors. For Barthes, it is language that speaks, not the author:

> the modern scriptor is born simultaneously with the text, is in no way equipped with a being preceding or exceeding the writing, is not the subject with the book as predicate; there is no other time than that of the enunciation and every text is eternally written here and now. . . . [The writer] traces a field without origin—or which, at least, has no other origin than language itself, language which ceaselessly calls into question all origins. . . . [A] text is not a line of words releasing a single 'theological' meaning (the 'message' of the Author-God) but a multi-dimensional space in which a variety of writings, none of them original, blend and clash. The text is a tissue of quotations drawn from the innumerable centers of culture. (145-46)[4]

Barthes is describing not so much the influence of particular books on authors but the influence of more intangible and amorphous cultural discourses. Yet, like Barthes, authors of the Middle Ages and the Renaissance, in their habit of recycling "olde bokes" and "cronikes," would also have perceived discourses as having lives of their own. Texts were seen not as products of autonomous authors but as revisionary reassemblages of prior texts.

The text of *Pericles* serves as an especially good case in point. The story probably originated in Greek romances, which in the Middle Ages were adapted in various Latin versions, including the *Historia Apollonii Regis Tyri* and the *Gesta Romanorum*. The *Historia* served as a source for Godfrey of Viterbo's *Pantheon*, which (as John Gower's Confessor tells us) served as a source for the Appolinus story in the *Confessio*, which served as a source for Shakespeare's *Pericles*—although parts of Shakespeare's play (especially Act 4, scenes 1, 3, 6) are indebted to Laurence Twine's *Patterne of Painefull Adventures* (c. 1576), which was derived from the Latin *Gesta*. (Significantly, the prologue to Twine's romance implicitly assumes the role of the author as mere mediator of preexistent stories: "Gathered into English by Laurence Twine"). To make matters even more intertextually complicated, Shakespeare's *Pericles* may be based at least partly on an earlier dramatic version of the story, a lost *Ur-Pericles*. Moreover, this complex web of adaptations and appropriations continues in George Wilkins' prose version of the story in *The Painfull Adventures of Pericles, Prince of Tyre* (1608), which apparently was derived from both Shakespeare's stage play and Twine's prose romance. As we can see in Godfrey, Gower, Twine, Shakespeare, and Wilkins, medieval and early modern authors did not autonomously create but rather intervened in fields of textuality which always preceded and exceeded the authority of any particular author. At any point in its textual lineage, the Appolinus/Pericles story could indeed be described in Roland Barthes' terms as "a tissue of quotations."

As an author of stage plays, Shakespeare would have found his authorial control limited and constrained. Plays were written under conditions of state censorship, requiring approval by the Master of Revels Office. As playwright, Shakespeare did not enjoy legal rights over his scripts; instead, plays became the property of the acting company. In the common practice of "continuous copy," plays were often revised or rewritten by other dramatists, or by the same dramatist at a later time. Indeed, several of Shakespeare's plays are likely the products of collaborative or mixed authorship (Taylor 335–36). Even actors in the process of rehearsal may have contributed to changes and revisions in the play script.

Moreover, in stage performances, Shakespeare's plays would have been subject to the manifold uncertainties and contingencies that flesh is heir to: the availability and variability of men and boy actors, as well as inevitable variations in the responses of different audiences. As playwright, Shakespeare must have repeatedly encountered dissonance between authorial intention and dramatic execution, compounded by often inexplicable differences in audience reception—a bewildering complex of variables almost entirely beyond Shakespeare's range of authorial control. While a text in print appears the same from day to day, performances on stage are always and inevitably different. Beyond authorial intentions—which might also be diverse and inconsistent—plays on stage would generate their own uncontrolled and uncontrollable excesses of performative meaningfulness.

Even Shakespeare's printed stage plays (in quarto editions) would have achieved a high degree of textual autonomy. Renaissance authors generally did not see their texts through the printing process; instead, printers assumed responsibility (or irresponsibility) for the production and layout of texts. Unlike plays on stage, printed editions of plays were entirely severed from the presence and directorial control of the author. Read in solitude (rather than seen in communion with other spectators), printed plays would be all the more susceptible to individual interpretations. Moreover, the rise of Protestant individualism, and the growing practice of private reading and study (made possible by mass-produced texts), would have exacerbated the tendency, as all texts (scriptural and otherwise) would have been subjected more and more to private readings and endless varieties of interpretative possibilities.

Yet in early modern England, such traditional conceptions of the author and such constraints upon authorial control were opposed and countered by the emergent forces of Renaissance individualism and capitalistic conceptions of authors as autonomous makers and owners of their texts. By mid-career Shakespeare had made a name for himself; indeed, he became the premier playwright for his company, a company in which he owned one of the ten shares. His literary and economic rise in prominence was complemented by, and most likely contributed to, his rise in social status when in 1596 his father's application for a coat of arms (and thus gentry status) was reactivated and approved. Shakespeare's literary prestige even spread beyond his own works in that texts he likely did not write, such as most of the poems in the *Passionate Pilgrim* (1599), were attributed to Shakespeare on the title page. Shakespeare did not only write popular plays, but developed, or more fully developed, modes of drama (such as history plays and romances) that other playwrights imitated and further developed. Thus Shakespeare's authority spread beyond his own texts to possess various derivative and imitative works. Moreover, Shakespeare lived in an intellectually and geographically expanding world, a world in which religious controversies, scientific empiricism, urban growth, and global trade placed ever-increasing demands on authors to produce new forms of literary expression. New authors gained cultural prestige as the world of early modern Europe could no longer be represented, or adequately represented, by the authority of old books.

Though Ben Jonson was the first playwright to publish his *Works* in the expensive and culturally prestigious format of a Folio edition in 1616, the posthumous publication of Shakespeare's plays in Folio soon followed in 1623. Along with Jonson, Shakespeare contributed mightily to the popularity and rising cultural status of plays which made such Folio editions economically profitable. Like Michelangelo inscribing his name on the *Pieta*, Shakespeare by late career could claim the cultural status of a self-possessed and autonomous artist.

Shakespeare lived and worked in a culture in which lingering traditional and emerging early-modern notions of the author coexisted—or rather persisted in tension. In *Pericles*, Shakespeare engages and responds to such conflicting notions of the author by bringing into prominence on stage the figure of the choric-authorial Gower. In the role of Gower, however, Shakespeare does not simply promote more modern notions of the author while countering medieval notions. On the contrary, one of the most prominent features of the choric Gower is that he seems especially old-fashioned and medieval. If the woodcut illustration of the choric Gower on the title page of Wilkins' *Painfull Adventures of Pericles* is a faithful rendition of Gower as he appeared on stage, he apparently wore an old-fashioned cap, wooden shoes, and held a staff and laurel (see Hoeniger, "Gower and Shakespeare" 463). In other words, "ancient Gower" (1.Chorus.2) looked ancient. Along with his archaic garb, Gower speaks in a contrived fourteenth-century idiom and an old-fashioned verse style of end-stopped, rhymed, tetrameter couplets. He also frequently appeals to the audience to accept antiquated literary conventions, and he continually comments on the play in highly didactic and moral terms. Indeed, the choric Gower seems at times more medieval than the medieval Gower.

Moreover, the choric Gower seems strangely at odds with the play he presents. In only one other play, *Henry V*, does Shakespeare make extensive use of a chorus; yet, the historical chorus is far more integrated into the play, speaking the same idiom and verse form as the other characters, and most likely wearing garments that are not particularly odd or old-fashioned. The choric Gower, however, seems disjointed from the play—standing, as he so well puts it, in the "gaps" (4.4.8). Gower certainly fulfills traditional choric obligations by introducing the action, providing background exposition, and keeping us abreast of the passages of time and the potentially bewildering shifts in location. Yet as a conventional chorus Gower seems unconventionally distanced from the play.

Though an author-choric figure, Gower insistently disclaims authority over the story he presents. He repeatedly reminds the audience of his literary indebtedness, that the story he presents is not his own: "To sing a song that old was sung, / From ashes ancient Gower is come," "It hath been sung at festivals," "And lords and ladies in their lives / Have read it for restoratives," "I tell you what mine authors say," "it is said / For certain in our story," "our story says" (1.Chorus.1–20, 4.Chorus.18–19, 5.Chorus.2). He offers himself as a subservient mediator for a literary and textual tradition that precedes and exceeds his own authority. Though the Confessor in the *Confessio* often mentions his sources as well, the chorus in the play seems not merely indebted to the textual traditions of the past, but apologetic for his poetic incompetence—"the lame feet of my rhyme" (4.Chorus.48)—and for his archaic limitations before an audience whose "wit's more ripe" (1.Chorus.12). He will manage, as he repeatedly says, only with the "patience" (4.4.50, 5.3.102) and "pardon" (2.Chorus.40, 4.4.5) of the audience. Though in the prologue to *Henry V*, the chorus also requests "pardon" since a wooden cockpit and a few actors cannot adequately represent whole armies and the fields of France, the choric Gower of *Pericles* insists not upon the limitations of the theater, but upon the limitations of the chorus.

The choric Gower not only mimics the language and verse form of the source but often exceeds the old-fashioned style of the source. Indeed, his aphoristic couplets often seem more rigid and more formulaic than the verse of the *Confessio*. Instead of animating and enlarging the play, Gower's commentary tends to constrain and limit the play into choric couplets of rigid moralization:

> Here have you seen a mighty king
> His child, I wis, to incest bring;
> A better prince and benign lord,
> That will prove aweful both in deed and word. (2.Chorus.1–4)

The choric Gower habitually reduces the dynamics of the play into simple proverbs:

> I'll show you those in trouble's reign,
> Losing a mite, a mountain gain. (2.Chorus.7–8)

While the chorus of *Henry V* attempts to overcome the constraints of the theater by urging the imaginative participation of the audience, Gower's commentary tends to reduce the action of the play into neatly balanced and overly deterministic rhymes. Yet if we feel unsatisfied with the quaint simplicities of Gower, so too does Gower. Indeed, he continually negates his own interpretive authority, as he deflects our attention from his choric presence to the play itself. Introducing the first dumb show, he aptly remarks, "What need I speak?" (2.Chorus.16), and then, as he spies the entrance of Pericles, he apologizes for his own intrusion, and defers to the authority of the text over his own choric authority (or rather lack of it):

> And here he comes. What shall be next,
> Pardon old Gower—this longs the text. (2.Chorus.39–40)

Not only does he beg our indulgence once again, but in the phrase "longs the text" Gower implies both that he needlessly *lengthens the text* and that what he has to say more properly *belongs to the text*. Though Gower is a most congenial guide and ever-helpful mediator between the audience and the sprawling, episodic play, nevertheless his authorial and interpretative commentary leaves something to be desired. Often his remarks devolve into a mere recording of the alternating ups and downs of Fortune:

> Till fortune, tired of doing bad
> Threw him ashore, to give him glad. (2.Chorus.37–38)

> But fortune, mov'd,
> Varies again; the grisled north
> Disgorges such a tempest forth. . . . (3.Chorus.46–48)

His poetic sensibilities remain habitually reductive and mechanistic. Indeed, when he does verge upon "grace" and "wonder," he seems quickly to scramble back onto solid ground, as when he introduces the mature Marina:

> . . . who hath gain'd
> Of education all the grace,
> Which makes her both the heart and place
> Of general wonder. But, alack,
> That monster Envy. . . . (4.Chorus.5–2)

The very instant "grace" and "wonder" enter his choric vocabulary, Gower turns upon the adversative conjunction "But," and proceeds to launch into a neat, balanced, antithetical account of "monster Envy."

Gower's gentle urging that we see in the play more than he sees, that we read beyond his reading, that we transcend his inept and naive poetic sensibilities, seems eminently necessary when we are confronted by his exceedingly formulaic closing commentary on the play:

> In Antiochus and his daughter you have heard
> Of monstrous lust the due and just reward.
> In Pericles, his queen and daughter, seen,
> Although assail'd with fortune fierce and keen,
> Virtue preserv'd from fell destruction's blast,
> Led on by heaven, and crown'd with joy at last.
> In Helicanus may you well descry
> A figure of truth, of faith, of loyalty.
> In reverend Cerimon there well appears
> The worth that learned charity aye wears.
> For wicked Cleon and his wife. . . . (5.3.86–96)

The final speech of the play is not ordinarily the place for the most profound and searching verse; nevertheless, Gower's attempt at closure not only fails to adequately close the play but seems strangely dissonant from the play. His choric summation misrepresents more than represents what we have seen on stage. In his overstrained effort to achieve balance and symmetry, Gower elevates distinctly minor characters, such as Helicanus and Cerimon, to major standing, while the climactic miracles of the final scenes are reduced, or rather overlooked, in the concluding sequence of end-stopped rhymed couplets. The sense of profound wonder that surfaces in the final act, as well as earlier in the play—"What world is this?," "Is not this strange?," "Most rare" (3.2.108–10)—seems conspicuously absent in the commentary of Gower. As chorus, Gower seems out of accord with the play, an author figure without authority or control over the text he presents.

Shakespeare's presentation of Gower seems not only at odds with the play but at odds with John Gower's presentation of Gower, or rather the Confessor-narrator who serves as the primary choric voice in the *Confessio*. Though the choric Confessor acknowledges his indebtedness to ancient and preexistent stories—"Of a cronike in daies gone. . . I rede thus," "as saith the boke," "To telle as olde bokes seyne," "as the cronikes seyne" (VIII, 279–81, 284, 1160, 1554)—he exercises considerably more authority over the story he tells. When the Confessor offers interpretive commentary on the story of Appolinus, his remarks, though never absolute or definitive, are closely integrated into the poem. He may seem at times preoccupied with the rhythmic irregularities of Fortune:

> Fortune hath ever be muable
> And maie no while stonde stable.
> For nowe it heith, nowe it loweth,
> Nowe stant upright, nowe overthroweth,
> Nowe full of blisse, and nowe of bale. (VIII, 593–97)

Yet, unlike the mechanistic and myopic chorus of the play, the Confessor also seems capable of a language of wonder and marvel:

> But for to speake of the mervailes
> Which afterwarde to him befelle,
> It is a wonder for to telle. (VIII, 984–86)

> At Ephesus the sea upcast
> The coffre, and all that was therin.
> Of great mervaile now begyn. . . . (VIII, 1164–66)

Far more than the chorus of the play, the choric Confessor apprehends a mysterious order that lurks beyond the shiftiness of Fortune. Moreover, the Confessor, though moral, is considerably less moralistic. His closing summation of the Appolinus narrative, though framed as a balanced contrast between noble Appolinus and wicked Antiochus, does not devolve into rigid formula:

> And in ensample his life was writte,
> That all lovers mighten witte
> Howe at laste it shal be sene
> Of love what thei wolden mene.
>   For see nowe on that other side,
> Antiochus with all his pride,
> Whiche sette his love unkyndely,
> His ende had sodeynly,
> Set ageyn kynde upon vengeance,
> And for his lust hath his penance. (VIII, 2007–2016)

Moral Gower, no doubt—but the verse here, as elsewhere in the *Confessio*, is rarely reductive or overly formulaic.

Though the Confessor, as priest of Venus, may not function as an authoritative voice at every moment in the poem (at times he seems argumentative and even uncertain in his counsel to Amantis), nevertheless his highly moral and didactic commentary seems generally reliable and in keeping with John Gower's didactic intentions as set forth in the prologue to the *Confessio*. Indeed, the authorial and didactic voice of John Gower's prologue seems periodically to resurface in the commentary of the Confessor, such as in the Confessor's introductory and concluding comments to the tale of Appolinus:

> Of that befill in tyme er this,
> The present tyme whiche nowe is
> Maie ben enformed, how it stoode,
> And take that hym, thynketh good,
> And leve that, whiche is nought so. (VIII, 261–65)

> Forthly my sonne I wolde the rede
> To let all other love aweie,
> But if it be through suche a weie,
> As love and reason wold accorde. (VIII, 2028–31)

Such remarks, though not particularly surprising or subtle, are in full accord with John Gower's overall didactic purposes in the poem.

Moreover, the Confessor's moral and choric commentary is consistently supplemented and endorsed by the various Latin texts in the *Confessio*: both the Latin verse epigrams and the more numerous and extensive Latin marginal glosses.[5] The Latin epigrams function primarily as introductory thematic overviews for each major section of the poem, as we see in the epigram that marks the beginning of the Appolinus story:

> Omnibus est communis amor, sed et immoderatos
> > Quae facit excessus, non reputatur amans.
> Sors tamen unde Venus attractat corda videre,
> > Quae rationis erunt, non ratione finit. (VIII, 275–78)

The general theme (that Love is common to all, but the immoderate and excessive lover is no true lover) may not seem especially surprising or profound, but certainly accords with and reinforces the moral voice of the Confessor, as well as the moral voice of the prologue. The more numerous Latin marginal glosses also offer occasional thematic guidance, but most often function as brief indices and guides to the plot. Yet when the poem mentions such mysteries as the intervening grace of God—

> But such a grace god hir sent,
> That for the sorowe, whiche she made,
> Was none of hem, which power hade
> To done hir any vilanie (VIII,1436–39)—

the accompanying Latin marginal gloss—"Qualiter Leoninus Thaisim ad lupanar destinavit, Ubi dei gracia preventa, ipsius virginitatem nullus violare potuit"—does not fail to convey and even enhance the theme of providential grace and protection. Though many of the Latin glosses add little beyond what we can find in the English text, they rarely seem inadequate or disjointed or at odds with the main text of the poem (indeed, many of the Latin glosses are so intimately connected to the poem that they simply translate key phrases from the English verse). Though the various Latin voices that frame the poem might possibly have suggested for Shakespeare the archaic voice of the chorus that frames the play, the effects of the Latin text ultimately seem quite different. While the choric Gower speaks an antiquated and often inadequate English, the Latin epigrams and glosses of the *Confessio* gain choric authority simply by virtue of being in Latin—a language of learning and cultural authority. Moreover, the Latin texts in the *Confessio* are not spoken by any character in the poem but rather appear as anonymous and disembodied voices, and thus all the more seemingly transcendent and authoritative. Even in the print format and layout of the medieval poem, the Latin verse headings and marginal glosses visually frame, hedge in, and tightly control the text. In effect, the choric Latin voices along with the cho-ric Confessor serve as highly integrated voices that mutually authorize and regulate the text. (Although, ironically, at the end of the *Confessio* we dis-cover that it is neither the Confessor nor the Latin voices but rather the an-guished lover Amantis who is identified as "John Gower"—a point to which I will return later.)[6]

In radical contrast to the authoritative choric voices that prevail over the source text, the choric Gower of the stage play remains distinctly distanced from and subordinate to the story he presents. Apologetic and self-effacing before an audience whose wits are more ripe, the choric Gower proves inca-pable of comprehending a play that exceeds his naive and unsophisticated grasp. As an author figure, or perhaps parody of an author figure, Gower dutifully transmits old stories with little interference and minimal compre-hension—although, as I will argue later in this chapter, Shakespeare's de-motion of the role of the choric-author figure also may suggest an implicit and roundabout promotion (and self-promotion) of the role of the author.

The inept choric Gower does not merely stand (or falter) in the "gaps" of the play but occasionally enters into the very fabric of the text. His discor-dant choric commentary is ironically integrated into the play in that the play is periodically discordant with itself. Repeatedly, the flow of the action (and how rarely it flows) comes to a sudden halt as characters pause to provide choric and moral commentary, and, as with the choric Gower, such remarks are usually off key, if not woefully insufficient. In other words, the play con-tains internal choruses that mimic the ineptitude of the external chorus. The three fishermen, for example, prove quite adept at extracting morality from fish. Fish live in the sea, the first fisherman expounds, "as men do a-land; the great ones eat up the little ones" (2.1.28–29). As Pericles is quick to respond, this seems "a pretty moral" (2.1.35). Yet the accuracy of such moralizing seems partial at best—suited to the daughter-devouring Antiochus, but fail-ing to account for the generosity of Pericles to Cleon, or the benign govern-ance of the good king Simonides, or even the kindness of the fishermen to Pericles and his kindness to them.

Consistently in the play, interpretations prove misinterpretations or under-interpretations. The white flags of Pericles' ships are wrongly interpreted by Cleon as signs of strategic deception. King Simonides' dissimulation with his daughter's letter is wrongly interpreted by Pericles as a scheme to undo him. Even the bawds in the brothel prove hermeneutic incompetents when they in-terpret Marina as a gift of fortune, only to find her more of a nuisance than a blessing, although eventually she does prove a profitable blessing, but in a way they never anticipated. All of these various misinterpretations, significantly, are Shakespeare's additions to the story—revisionary embellishments upon the Appolinus story in the *Confessio*.

Shakespeare also adds to the play an entire scene, without precedent in the *Confessio*, that is focused directly on issues of interpretation. King Simonides systematically interprets and comments upon a series of emblematic shields presented by various knights. At the end of the line Pericles enters, holding a "withered branch, that's only green at top" (2.2.43). The king renders a prompt, insightful, and self-confident interpretation:

> A pretty moral;
> From the dejected state wherein he is,
> He hopes by you his fortunes yet may flourish. (2.2.45–47)

Simonides seems to hit upon the meaning, perhaps even the precise meaning that Pericles intended. Yet, the meaning of the "withered branch" is not ultimately fixed or settled by Simonides, but continues to exfoliate throughout the play, developing a semiotic richness that well exceeds any single interpretive configuration. By Act 5, the branch that is "green at top" comes to suggest not merely Pericles' restoration of his fortunes through marriage to Simonides' daughter, but his later reunion with his supposedly deceased daughter, as well as his subsequent reunion with his wife in Diana's temple, along with his recovery of his mental and spiritual health, and even the political growth and expansion of his empire (to include not only Tyre but Pentapolis). Indeed, the branch well exceeds Simonides' reading of the branch. Like the choric Gower, the choric Simonides fails to comprehend or restrain the proliferating free play of meanings that evolve in the play.

The tendency in the play for characters to speak in a Gower-like mode of less-than-authoritative choric authority is perhaps most evident in Pericles himself as he habitually pauses to interpret, or rather misinterpret, his experiences. After washing ashore in Pentapolis, for instance, he describes himself as a tennis ball randomly knocked about in the "vast tennis court" (2.1.60) of the sea. Yet within minutes he discovers that his father's rusty armor has been not-so-randomly recovered in a fishing net. He then scrambles to reinterpret his experience: "Thanks, fortune, yet, that, after all my crosses, / Thou givest me somewhat to repair myself" (2.1.123–24). Yet even this reinterpretation proves merely another in an ongoing series of interpretations of the nature of fortune and the sea.

Indeed, the enigmatic sea—an almost constant presence in the play—evolves as a recurrent metaphor that continually eludes final interpretation. The protean sea assumes a dizzying array of manifestations: tennis racket-wielding Neptune, mother goddess and redeemer, angry tempest, sea of tranquility, giver and taker of life, divider and reuniter of families, as well as home to kings, maidens, and pirates. Especially in the early modern world, the sea—in its geographical expansiveness—would suggest a realm of mystery and wonder, beyond final definition or knowledge. Even the more solid and substantial "ooze" (3.1.60) in which Thaisa is deposited suggests an elusive and indefinite fluidity. Appropriately, the god of the sea is described as "mask'd Neptune" (3.3.38)—hidden, inscrutable, beyond full comprehension.[7]

A sense of irreducible enigma is introduced in the opening scene of the play, not just in the riddle, which seems surprisingly unenigmatic (especially compared to the more challenging riddle of the *Confessio*), but in the persistently enigmatic and slippery world that confronts Pericles. In the opening scene, Pericles, before interpreting the riddle, interprets the face of the princess of Antioch—and gets it all wrong:

> See where she comes, appareled like the spring,
> Graces her subjects, and her thoughts the king
> Of every virtue gives renown to men!
> Her face the book of praises, where is read
> Nothing but curious pleasures. (1.1.16–17)

Pericles soon realizes, however, that her pleasures have been a bit too curious, and so he is compelled to reread and reinterpret the outward significance of the daughter's beauty: "this glorious casket stor'd with ill" (1.1.78). He likewise misinterprets the music of Antioch as heavenly and divine music—mistakes it, in other words, for the music of the spheres that will sound in Act 5. As an internal and inept chorus within the play, Pericles repeatedly misreads or underreads the texts of his world.

Moreover, Pericles underinterprets the death's heads that hang as iconic and emblematic riddles on the wall in Antioch. He sees them merely as a reminder of human mortality, a conventional *memento mori*: "For death remembered should be like a mirror, / Who tells us life's but breath, to trust it error" (1.1.46–47).[8] Pericles neglects to see any further association between the heads on the wall and the amorous impulses that drove him to Antioch. The heads of the failed suitors, however, may pose a riddle not just of human mortality but of the intimacy or potential intimacy between love and death, signifying, in other words, that illicit love leads to sterility and death. Pericles' "inflam'd desire . . . To taste the fruit of yon celestial tree" (1.1.21–22) suggests an allegorical reenactment of the Fall of Man. Though Pericles makes a hasty exit, never actually tasting the fruit, he verges upon sin by mistaking a lesser good for a greater good, attempting to find in the face of the princess—"beyond all wonder" (1.2.76)—a substitute for the wonders of heavenly paradise.

Pericles' shrewd decoding of the riddle of Antioch may function in the play not as a confirmation of his role as authoritative and reliable interpreter, but as a foil to his tendency to misread and underread the more elusive riddles that confront him. Though Antiochus is impressed with Pericles' hermeneutic skill—"He hath found the meaning" (1.1.144)—Pericles, like Oedipus, seems to untangle the riddle of the sphinx only to ignore the riddles in his own life.

Indeed, the subsequent scene strongly suggests that Pericles may have failed to fully resolve the riddle of Antioch. When he returns to Tyre, he enters the stage bemoaning for thirty-three lines his condition of "dull-ey'd melancholy" that "Makes both my body and soul to languish" (1.2.2, 32), and he expresses bewilderment for lack of any clear and discernable cause. He proceeds to consider, and quickly dismiss, a series of speculative causes for his melancholy, until finally he settles on what he takes to be the definitive root cause—fear of a military invasion by Antiochus. Yet as a master of riddles, Pericles' interpretation of his aching melancholy seems remarkably unsubtle. Moreover, his melancholy is distinctly Shakespeare's addition to the story. In the *Confessio*, melancholy is felt not by Appolinus, but by the citizens of Tyre after they hear of his departure:

> Whan that thei wist he was ago,
> It is a pitee for to here.
> They losten lust, they losten chere,
> They toke upon hem suche penance,
> There was no song, there was no daunce,
> But every myrthe and melodie
> To hem was then a maladie. (VIII, 484–88)

In effect, Shakespeare displaces the melancholy in his source from the citizens of Tyre to Pericles. The play thus renders the cause of Pericles' melancholy rather curious and problematic, for while the citizens in the poem have a clear and certain cause for their despondency, Pericles does not. Yet since his melancholy follows immediately after his departure from Antioch, his despondency seems linked, dramatically and psychologically, to his encounter with incest. His revulsion in Antioch—"my thoughts revolt" (1.1.72)—may emerge not merely from his discovery of putrefaction in his object of desire (the princess), but also from an unrecognized putrefaction in his own desire. The "danger, which [he] fear'd, is at Antioch" (1.2.7) may not, after all, be confined to Antioch, but may be lurking in himself, in a hid-

den and irrational obsession with incest—an enigmatic "sea" in his own nature. His melancholy, which he is quick to interpret and define, seems far
more mysterious, far more of a riddle, than he comprehends.

Pericles' desire to find in the princess a "boundless happiness" (1.1.25)
may indicate as well an unacknowledged longing for an illicit boundary-
crossing happiness. An excessive passion also characterizes the hero of the
Confessio as he sets sail for Antioch:

> Appolinus the prince of Tyre,
> Whiche hath to love a great desire,
> As he whiche in his high moode,
>   Was likinge of his hote blode,
> A yonge, a freshe, a lustie knyght. . . .
> To ship he goeth, the winde him driveth. (VIII, 383–93)

"Great desire," "Hote blode," and "winde" are conventional markers of unhinged and dangerous passions. A troubled sexuality also seems indicated in
Appolinus when he leaves his daughter with Stangulio and Dionyse (Cleon
and Dionyza), pledging never again to shave until his daughter is married:

> And this avowe to god I make,
> That I shall never for hir sake
> My berde for no likynge shave,
> Till it befalle, that I have
> In covenable tyme of age
> Besette hir unto mariage. (VIII, 1309–14)

He will not shave "for her sake." Such a course of action seems curious, to
say the least, and might suggest, whether Gower intended it or not, a fear in
the hero of an incestuous fate, a fate that can best be avoided by assuming an
uncouth and undesirable appearance until his daughter is wed and he is in the
clear.

Shakespeare may have read, or misread, the *Confessio* as suggesting an
incest anxiety in the hero.[9] Indeed, the play develops and expands upon such
possibilities:

> Till she be married, madam,
> By bright Diana, whom we honor, all
> Unscissor'd shall this hair of mine remain,
> Though I show ill in 't. (3.3.29–32)

Pericles' vow to grow his hair is directed to Diana, thus becoming, implicitly, a vow of chastity to the goddess of chastity. Pericles vows to grow his hair, assume the form of a ragged outcast, and live chaste until his daughter marries. The goddess Diana, barely mentioned in the poem, emerges as a key figure in the play. Diana is prayed to by Marina in the brothel, and even appears to Pericles in a dream (an anonymous god appears in the poem). Apparently, the goddess of chastity not only protects Marina from the desires of the brothel customers, but also protects Pericles from potentially incestuous desires in himself.

In the final act, Shakespeare continues to develop and expand upon the various suggestions of incestuous desire in the source text. In the *Confessio*, Appolinus and his daughter are reunited in an atmosphere highly conducive to sexual indiscretion: the "yonge Thaise" enters alone into Appolinus' cabin, "so derke a place," to play music and "By all the weies, that she can,/ To glad with this sory man" (VIII, 1649–70). In his solipsistic despair, Appolinus rejects her and even strikes her with his hand. Thaise then defends herself with an appeal to her noble lineage, an appeal that may evoke suggestions of courtship:

> Avoy my lorde, I am a mayde,
> And if ye wyst, what I am,
> And out of what linage I cam,
> Ye wolde not be so salvage. (VIII, 1704–07)

In Shakespeare's play, Pericles is reunited with his daughter in a scene that develops even further an atmosphere of wooing and seduction. Like Leontes, who gazes unknowingly upon his own daughter as a potential new mate—"I'd beg your precious mistress, / Which he counts but a trifle" (*Winter's Tale* 5.1.223–24)—Pericles finds his daughter appealing for her strong resemblance to his lost wife: "for thou lookest / Like one I loved indeed" (5.1.127–28). When Pericles pushes her away, Marina responds by appealing not only to her noble lineage but to her beauty, modesty, and power to elicit desire:

> I am a maid, my lord, that ne'er before
> Invited eyes, but have been gazed on
> Like a comet. . . .
> My derivation was from ancestors
> Who stood equivalent with mighty kings. (5.1.87–94)

When Pericles finally recognizes Marina, he responds in language strongly
suggesting erotic rapture:

> O Helicanus, strike me, honor'd sir,
> Give me a gash, put me to present pain,
> Lest this great sea of joys rushing upon me
> O'erbear the shores of my mortality,
> And drown me with their sweetness. O, come hither,
> Thou that beget'st him that did thee beget. (5.1.195–200)

The cryptic final line, in which Pericles sees himself as both father and son to
his daughter, recalls the perverse family relations in the opening scene in
Antioch. Likewise, the highly evasive and riddling language of Marina (earlier in the scene) associates her with the daughter of Antioch.[10] Yet once
again Pericles overcomes the degrading threat of an erotics of incest, and instead moves towards a transcendent erotics of faith, in which he and his
daughter evoke not the perversions of Antioch but the Christian mystery in
which Christ proves, paradoxically, both father and son to his mother. Marina,
a name repeatedly associated with the sea, now calls for reinterpretation in association with the celestial Mary, the virgin mother/daughter of her
son/father.

Sea imagery returns once again, with insistent repetition—"great sea of
joys," "shores of my mortality," "drown me," "Thou that wast born at sea,
buried at Tharsus, / And found at sea again!" (5.1.197–202). A wondrous
and inexplicable sea delivers Pericles from the threat of incest, and redeems
him from his desperate melancholy. This wonder of unexpected grace is then
redoubled in the "great miracle" (5.3.59) of the final scene when Pericles is
finally reunited with his wife in Diana's temple—and thus the riddles in the
play continue to unfold and further unfold.

By tracing a series of incestuous implications in the text, I do not mean to
suggest that Pericles should be seen as a latent pervert who deserves all the
suffering he gets until he is purged of wayward desires. Indeed, how can we
fault Pericles for not acknowledging in Act 1 a potentially incestuous desire for
a daughter he does not conceive until Act 3? My point is not that incest functions as a master code that renders the text fully readable, but rather that incestuous desire lurks in the text as an elusive possibility, a possibility that belies the
hasty and overly confident interpretations of Pericles, as well as the reductive
and simplistic commentaries of the choric Gower. The riddle of incest that confronts Pericles in Act 1 is not definitively unraveled and left behind in Antioch,
but continues to surface in the linguistic richness and free play of the text, despite the myopic limitations of the internal chorus, Pericles, and the external

chorus, Gower. Beyond the riddle of Antioch lurks the riddle of Pericles, which neither Pericles nor Gower can ever fully contain or resolve.

The play continually depicts Gower, along with the internal choruses, at odds with the dynamics of the text. Choric interpretations consistently devolve into misinterpretations and underinterpretations, as the text continues to elude all choric formulations of the text. The choric commentary of Gower functions not as a fixed and secure hermeneutic frame for the play, but as an inept and myopic foil to a text that proves too slippery and suggestive for choric authority and control.

As presenter of a text that exceeds his authority, Gower serves at least in part as a confession of Shakespeare's own authorial limitations. Yet, ironically, Gower may also function as a strategic claim to authorial control and mastery of quite another sort. Complementing the author's inability to control and restrain free-floating textuality is the author's ability to convey and mediate free-floating textuality. Perhaps the greatest of all miracles in *Pericles* is that Gower, in spite of his myopic limitations, manages to present a play that aspires to transcendent and timeless truth—even if the moments of transcendence remain entirely outside his choric field of vision. The inept Gower presents the play, and the play produces a bounty of surplus meaningfulness that well exceeds Gower's intentions. The play does not, in other words, pronounce the death of the author—or rather the stillbirth of the author as he emerged in early modern Europe—but rather makes a discreet claim to authorial elevation and even mystification. In effect, Shakespeare's use of Gower involves a double strategy: an explicit demotion of the author as mere mediator of texts he cannot comprehend or control, and an implicit promotion of the author as mediator of texts that transcend all human comprehension and control. Like Gower the chorus, Shakespeare the author serves as humble mediator through which old stories are told and retold, and yet, in spite of all limitations, Shakespeare also serves as authorial medium through which eternal and divine truth speaks. Thus the closest analogy in the *Confessio* to the choric Gower of the play may be neither the Confessor nor the Latin voices, but the inept and confused Amantis—the least competent speaker in the poem, and yet the figure who in the end is identified as "John Gower." If the "John Gower" of the poem's conclusion is a surrogate for John Gower the author, then the author Gower also seems to suggest that in spite of his own authorial limitations he can nevertheless manage to convey and transmit the theological and moral truths of the *Confessio*.[11]

I would conclude with a final glance at Shakespeare's play, the moment when Pericles finds in Marina, even before he recognizes her, a truth transcending his desperate and confused melancholy:

thou lookest
Modest as Justice, and thou seemest a palace
For the crown'd Truth to dwell in. (5.1.123–25)

Yet thou dost look
Like Patience gazing on king's graves, and smiling
Extremity out of act. (5.1.140–42)

Beyond Pericles' muddled vision shimmers transcendent and Platonic truth—a beatific vision of Marina transfigured from fleshly self to radiant symbol of eternal virtues: Justice, Truth, Patience. It is one of several hieratic moments in the play when the shadowy world of existence figures forth a realm of pure essence.

It is a moment that Pericles barely understands, and that Gower the chorus seems to miss altogether. Outside Gower's field of vision, the text claims to offer a glimmer of divine and eternal truth. Though Gower falls short in his role as controller and interpreter of the text, he succeeds nonetheless as a mediator of truths beyond his own frail apprehension. Indeed, his lack of understanding may even serve as testimony to the supreme value of the truth he presents—for the truth of the text proves too rarefied for ordinary or even choric-authorial comprehension. Through the use of Gower as surrogate author, Shakespeare reduces the role of the author to humble and unknowing mediator while also mystifying the role of the author as medium through which absolute and even divine truth speaks—if not loud and clear, then at least through a textual glass darkly. In a strategic move that finds its counterpart in Ben Jonson's rather bold publication of his *Works* in Folio (an implicit claim to literary standing), Shakespeare, a man who succeeded in elevating his civic status to that of gentleman, aspires beyond the craft of playwrighting to a mystique of literary transcendence.

Notes

1. For these and other early responses to *Pericles*, see Hoeniger, Introduction lxix–lxxi; and Bullough 6: 349.

2. For studies of Shakespeare's use of the choric Gower in *Pericles*, see Hoeniger, "Gower and Shakespeare" 461–79; Semon 17–27; Eggers 434–43; and Hillman 427–37. I am indebted to all these articles, though none takes the approach of the present chapter, which is to examine the role of the choric Gower in relation to the various choric and authorial voices in the *Confessio*. Except where otherwise noted, all references to the *Confessio* in this chapter are from *Narrative and Dra-*

matic Sources, vol. 6. For the complete *Confessio Amantis*, see the edition by G. C. Macaulay.

3. Except for a few general comments, I do not intend to deal with (or resolve) the sticky issues concerning Shakespeare's authorship of *Pericles*. The old-fashioned style of the play, and the fact that it was not printed in the First Folio, has led several scholars to suspect collaborative or mixed authorship. Most scholars accept Acts 3–5 as predominantly the work of Shakespeare, but some contend that Acts 1–2 are predominantly the work of another playwright. I would argue that if Shakespeare rewrote an old play, or brought to completion an incomplete play, he clearly took pains to appropriate the archaic style of the earlier text into his revisionary reworking or completion of the play. The three dumb shows in Acts 1–2, for instance, are complemented by two additional dumb shows in Acts 3–5. Likewise, the choric Gower appears twice in the first two acts, but six times in the later acts (three times in Act 5 alone)—and though he speaks more lines of "Shakespearean" pentameter in his later appearances, his language remains archaic. Moreover, the loose structure and improbable events of the early acts are followed by even more loose structure and thoroughly impossible events later in the play. For studies of the play's deliberately archaic and medieval designs, see Hoeniger, "Gower and Shakespeare" 461–79; and Felperin, *Shakespearean Romance* 143–76.

4. Also see Michel Foucault, "What Is an Author?" 101–20. Foucault's essay (published one year after Barthes' "Death of the Author") argues not only that authors are the byproducts of cultural discourses, but that the very notion of an author is a cultural and artificial construction—an attempt to limit and control the potentially endless free play of textual meanings.

5. The Latin glosses of the *Confessio* in Bullough's *Narrative and Dramatic Sources* are printed not in the margins but inserted between passages of the English poem. For a more accurate and authentic reproduction of the Latin marginal glosses, see the text of the *Confessio* in Macaulay's edition. As with many medieval glosses, the glosses in the *Confessio* may not be the work of the author—although several recent scholars have argued that the glosses in the *Confessio* do appear to be the work of Gower (see Yeager 255). Whether the glosses were the work of Gower or not, I assume that Shakespeare read them as integral parts of the text.

6. Toward the end of the *Confessio*, Venus gives Amantis a "Peire of Bedes blak as Sable," and then addresses him as "John Gower" (see Book VIII, 2904–08 in Macaulay's edition). John Gower's strategy of making Amantis/John Gower the least authoritative voice in the poem not only resembles Chaucer's ironic strategy of presenting "Chaucer" as the naive narrator who tells the most inane and incompetent tale, but may have suggested Shakespeare's use of the inept choric-author figure of Gower in the play.

7. For a discussion of "mask'd Neptune," see Barber and Wheeler, *The Whole Journey* 311.

8. For a study of the iconic heads and other iconic stage images in the play, see Dunbar 86–97.

9. For a study of literary influence as a process of an author "misreading" his predecessor, see Bloom, *Anxiety* 19–45. Bloom argues that only poets after Milton felt such anxiety, but I would argue that such tendencies can be found in Shakespeare as well.

10. As Coppelia Kahn remarks, Marina's "oblique, cryptic, enigmatic mode of speech links her to the riddling, incestuous princess of Antioch" (232).

11. From a quite different perspective, Steven Mullaney also sees in *Pericles* an implicit claim to authorial transcendence. Examining the play in light of the location of the Globe theater in the marginal and disreputable suburban "Liberties" of London, Mullaney concludes that "*Pericles* represents a radical effort to dissociate the popular stage from its cultural contexts and theatrical grounds of possibility—an effort to imagine, in fact, that popular drama could be a purely aesthetic phenomenon, free from history and from historical determination" (147).

CHAPTER 5

Language in *Pandosto* and *The Winter's Tale*

In the trial scene, Hermione defends herself with a remark that highlights one of the most problematic features of *The Winter's Tale*: "Sir, / You speak a language that I understand not" (3.2.79–80). The language of Leontes seems unusually if not uniquely troublesome—among the most difficult and obscure passages in all thirty-seven plays.[1] Indeed a profound concern with language seems to persist throughout the play, from the deranged speeches of Leontes, to the more simple and concrete language of the Bohemian shepherds, to the nonlanguage of gesture and silence in the final scene. Yet the primary source on which the play is based, Robert Greene's *Pandosto: The Triumph of Time* (printed 1588, 1592, 1595, 1607), manifests virtually none of the problems or concerns with language that persist in the stage play. On the contrary, Greene's romance seems consistently to uphold language as a fully reliable medium of representation. The romance is narrated throughout in a highly refined and idealized language of euphuistic prose, with orderly and often symmetrical patterns of antithesis, alliteration, repetition, and occasionally rhyme. In rewriting the source text, Shakespeare does not merely refashion the outmoded language of the euphuistic romance into the contemporary blank verse and prose of the stage, but consistently seems to rupture and violate the very language and rhetorical fabric of the source. Like Shakespeare's other sources, Greene's *Pandosto* is not a neutral text, not a mere quarry for plot and character, but a text wrought with implicit assumptions—particularly assumptions about the nature and viability of language. In refashioning the source text into a stage play, Shakespeare does not merely borrow selectively, adjust for generic differences, and artfully improve upon the source, but writes against the linguistic assumptions of the source text.[2]

Shakespeare's concern with the nature of language in the play, however, is not exclusively in response to the elegant and refined language of the primary source text. Rather both texts are embedded in larger cultural controversies and debates about the nature of language in early modern Europe. Along with a general unsettling of long-held ideas about astronomy, politics, religion, gender, and so forth, the very nature of language was widely debated and contested throughout the Renaissance. Among a wide array of various and conflicting views, two opposing camps tended to emerge: a more traditional and Biblical view of language as intimately and organically linked to the world, and an emerging skeptical view of language as entirely arbitrary and slippery, degraded from any original Edenic connection with nature. Though the controversy was not entirely new—and indeed can be traced back to the opposing views of nominalists and realists in the Middle Ages—nevertheless in the sixteenth century the old debate gathered new energy, fueled by the new learning and the rise of scientific empiricism.

As a general tendency, in the early Renaissance more traditional views of language prevailed. Language, though degraded from the effects of Babel, was seen as largely reformed by the compensating gift of tongues at Pentecost. Early Renaissance humanists, such as Cornelius Agrippa, argued that even though many words had degenerated into purely arbitrary signifiers, some words still retained their original purity and intimate connection to real things in nature.[3] Other humanists claimed that although languages had degraded over time, as classical Latin had devolved into medieval scholastic Latin, a rigorous campaign of education could restore such languages to their original wholesomeness and integrity. Even as late as 1667, Thomas Sprat in *The History of the Royal Society* echoed the early linguistic reformers when he urged the learned community to "return back to the primitive purity and shortness, when men deliver'd so many things, almost in an equal number of words" (qtd. in Donawerth 126). At the subtextual heart of Thomas Sprat's call for linguistic reform is the traditional Biblical assumption of a fall into Babel that can be remedied by the gift of Pentecost—although for Sprat the gift of Pentecost was to take the form of scientific linguistic precision. Some Renaissance humanists even argued that the arbitrary nature of language can offer certain benefits, enabling speakers to assign names figuratively to things or ideas that do not yet have names; thus, if language lapses into metaphorical imprecisions, language compensates in its wondrous capacity for metaphorical flexibility and adaptability.[4]

By the late sixteenth and early seventeenth centuries, however, opposing views of language were gaining ground. Scientists and philosophical skeptics tended to see language as chronically fallen and degraded. Frequent rallying cries arose for the reform of language (as in Francis Bacon and the Royal Society), along with more radical calls for the invention of new and improved scientific languages or even the abandonment of language in favor of a denotative nonlanguage of mathematical notation (see DeGrazia 380). Such profound distrust of language is perhaps best expressed in the skepticism of Montaigne:

> Our speech has its weaknesses and its defects, like all the rest. Most of the occasions for the troubles of the world are grammatical. Our lawsuits spring only from debate over the interpretation of the laws, and most of our wars from the inability to express clearly the conventions and treaties of agreement of princes. How many quarrels, and how important, have been produced in the world by doubt of the meaning of that syllable *Hoc*! ("Apology for Raymond Sebond" 392)

According to Montaigne, even educated and reformed language—or rather especially educated and reformed language—suffers from the irreparable effects of Babel. As premodern post-structuralist, Montaigne insists upon the slippery and elusive nature of language in which meanings are chronically imprecise and endlessly deferred:

> Men do not know the natural infirmity of their mind: it does nothing but ferret and quest, and keeps incessantly whirling around, building up and becoming entangled in its own work, like our silkworms, and is suffocated in it. . . . Our disputes are purely verbal. I ask what is "nature," "pleasure," "circle," "substitution." The question is one of words, and is answered in the same way. "A stone is a body." But if you pressed on: "And what is a body?"—"Substance."—"And what is substance?" and so on, you would finally drive the respondent to the end of his lexicon. We exchange one word for another word, often more unknown. . . . To satisfy one doubt, they give me three; it is the Hydra's head. ("Of Experience" 817–19)[5]

Unlike the early linguistic reformers, Montaigne, at least in his more radical moments, finds language hopelessly unstable, not a solid vessel of truth but a slippery medium of self-deception and endless deferment.[6]

As a general pattern, Greene's *Pandosto* upholds and endorses a more traditional, Pentecostal view of language. The idealized euphuistic prose of the romance aspires to full authentic representation of the world, a reliable and unblemished mirror held up to nature. Even more, the highly balanced and symmetrical rhetorical structures of Greene's narrative faithfully reflect the corresponding orderliness in the designs of Fortune and Providence. Indeed, the implicit unity between the structures of euphuistic language and the structures of providential designs is previewed in the very phrasing of the preface:

> Pandosto. The Triumph of Time. Wherein is discovered by a pleasant Histo-
> rie, that although by the meanes of sinister fortune, Truth may be concealed
> yet by Time in spight of fortune it is most manifestly revealed. (156)

"Truth" may be for a time "concealed," but in a neatly balanced antithesis it will be (with the dependable assurance of a symmetrical rhyme) ultimately "revealed." The ordered, balanced, antithetical phrasing of Greene's preface reflects the orderliness of the overall narrative, and, even more, the orderliness and symmetry of providential justice. Greene's rhetoric aspires to full and precise mimetic representation of the ultimate providential schemes of even-handed justice in which transgressions are inevitably followed by a balanced countermovement of due punishment. With untroubled mimetic confidence, Greene narrates his story in a highly reformed and stylized language—in effect, a highly Pentecostal language that faithfully reflects nature and at times seems intimately woven into the very fabric of the universe.[7]

One of the most prominent rhetorical patterns in the romance is in the antithetical structure of events, as joy alternates with grief in accordance with the fickle (though quite regular and dependably fickle) mood swings of Fortune. Repeatedly, good fortune is followed by bad fortune, and the moments of transition are marked by such neatly balanced (and delightful) clauses as the following:

> Fortune minding to be wonton, willing to shewe that as she hath wrincles on
> her browes, so she hath dimples in her cheekes. (173)

> Fortune, who al this while had shewed a frendly face, began now to turne her
> back, and shewe a lowring countenance. (176)

Such balanced antithetical reversals (first anticipated in the prologue) continue to recur throughout the narrative. The romance, for instance, begins with a sequence of joys piled upon joys, followed by a countersequence of griefs piled upon griefs. Pandosto, we are told, has been victorious in war and courteous in peace, and thus appropriately rewarded with a marriage to

Bellaria, a woman royal, learned, fair, and virtuous. The combined virtues of the royal couple then inspire Fortune to bestow even greater bounty:

> They had not beene married long, but Fortune (willing to increase their happiness) lent them a sonne, so adorned with the gifts of nature, as the perfection of the Childe greatly augmented the love of the parentes, and the joys of their commons. (157)

The moment of fortunate climax, however, is soon followed by an inevitable and counterbalanced decline:

> Fortune envious of such happy successe, willing to shewe some signe of her inconstancie, turned her wheele, and darkened their bright sunne of prosperitie, with the mistie cloudes of mishap and misery. (157)

Fortune's meteorological mood swing induces a corresponding mood swing in the mind of the king who then gradually and methodically succumbs to suspicious jealousy.

Mad jealousy in the source text operates by the dictates of euphuistic prose, pursuing its effects with remarkable patience and well-ordered rhythm. King Pandosto only gradually suspects Queen Bellaria, and only after an accumulation of weighty, though quite circumstantial, evidence:

> Bellaria (who in her time was the flower of courtesie), willing to show how unfaynedly shee looved her husband by his friends interainment, used him likewise so familiarly . . . oftentimes comming her selfe into his bed chamber. (158)

Only after several such visitations does Pandosto feel the stirrings of jealousy: "This custome still continuing betwixt them, a certaine melancholy passion entring the minde of Pandosto, drave him into sundry and doubtfull thoughts" (158). In a gradually intensifying process, Fortune continues to turn her wheel, increasing the passions of the king. Apparently, days or even weeks pass before Pandosto begins "at last to kindle in his minde a secret mistrust, which increased by suspicion, grewe at last to be a flaming Jealousie, that so tormented him as he could take no rest" (159). The process is as orderly and methodical as the fire imagery in which it is couched: his passion was first kindled, then increased, then grew, and finally tormented. Mad jealousy disrupts the calm of Pandosto's court, but only in the form of neatly arranged, well-ordered rhetorical units.

In the stage play, Shakespeare appropriates many of the symmetries and balances of the romance (as evidenced in the two-part structure of the play, and the various contrasts between Sicily and Bohemia, winter and spring, age and youth, royalty and common folk, etc.), but at the same time Shakespeare ruptures and subverts the linguistic fabric of the source text. With a sense of language more akin to Montaigne than Agrippa, Shakespeare defies the cohesive, orderly, and fully comprehensible rhetorical structures of the romance. In contrast to King Pandosto, King Leontes suffers a reversal of fortune that develops quite suddenly, without apparent cause or adequate explanation. Interpretations of Leontes' jealousy abound in the play—tremor cordis, excess choler, a curse, the influence of some ill planet—but such conjectures become increasingly numerous and thus decreasingly credible, and the underlying cause remains stubbornly elusive.

In opposition to the source, the language of the play seems remarkably inconclusive and slippery, not a stable and deterministic language that can mirror the very structure of the universe. Language begins to break down particularly in the early speeches of Leontes. While in the romance the jealous king thinks and speaks in an eminently lucid and orderly prose, the language of Leontes becomes chronically distorted and deranged. His notoriously difficult speech on "Affection" seems an outpouring not only of a suspicious and enraged mind but of language itself gone awry in a frenzy of ruptured structure, inexplicable logic, and unruly suggestions:

> Can thy dam?—may 't be?—
> Affection, thy intention stabs the center.
> Thou dost make possible things not so held,
> Communicat'st with dreams—how can this be?—
> With what's unreal thou coactive art,
> And fellow'st nothing. Then 'tis very credent
> Thou mayst cojoin with something; and thou dost,
> And that beyond commission, and I find it,
> And that to the infection of my brains
> And hardening of my brows. (1.2.137–46)

Small wonder that Polixenes responds, "What means Sicilia?" (1.2.146). When Leontes asks "Can thy dam?—may 't be?," what is he referring to? The possibility of Hermione's adultery? The possible illegitimacy of even Mamillius? Or something else that Leontes keeps to himself? Whose affection stabs the "center"? Hermione's? Polixenes'? Leontes'? Is the "center" Leontes' heart that suffers from tremor cordis, or Hermione's sexual center stabbed by Polixenes, or might "center" suggest the earth as the center, or rather noncenter, of the defunct Ptolemaic universe? What or who "cojoins with something"? Does Hermione "cojoin" with Polixenes in an illicit affair, beyond license and commission? Or does Leontes' own affection stir up obscene fantasies that "cojoin" with the material world—the dream thus (in a parody of ontological proof) becoming strong and credent evidence of an actual affair? Or something else? What is the "nothing" that mysteriously produces "something"? The nothing (*ex nihilo*) out of which God created the universe, and out of which (in a perverse act of miscreation) Leontes conjures up his own world of deranged fantasy? Or is "nothing" a pun suggesting female genitalia, Hermione's absence and void, that Polixenes obscenely fills with his "something," as infected and as hard as the cuckold's horn Leontes imagines protruding from his own brows? And is there more in this?[8]

Such dizzying possibilities never emerge in Greene's text, where meanings are more clearly determinable, or at least more narrowly confined. Unlike his jealous but fully lucid counterpart, Leontes seems hopelessly immersed in an uncontrollable profusion of syntactic and semantic possibilities, a nightmare of sliding and wildly excessive signification. If Hermione seems "slippery" (1.2.272), it is in part because language itself becomes slippery. In contrast to the supremely cohesive language of the source, the language of the play degenerates into an unruly and depraved instrument of human misperception. In the mind of Leontes, language becomes complicit in his perverse vision of the world as a "bawdy planet" (1.2.201). Even his casual reference to the earth as "planet" evokes a wayward slipperiness at the heart of things: the earth, as one of the centers that "intention stabs," turns out to be a planet, a wanderer, a noncenter. Cosmologically and linguistically, the center is lost, or rather exposed as nonexistent. Without fixed or secure points of reference, every word and gesture, every signifier, slips and wanders about in Leontes' mind, producing wild surmises and endless profusions of interpretive possibilities. Like Montaigne's silkworm, Leontes incessantly whirls around, building up and becoming entangled in his own language.

Moreover, the infidelities of language in the play do not simply follow as a consequence of the imagined infidelities of Hermione, but seem complicit in miscreating the perception of Hermione as adulterous. Indeed the infidelities of language seem to spark Leontes' jealousy from the very start. Early in Act 1.2, Leontes apparently steps aside from Hermione and Polixenes (since for over fifty lines he says nothing, while his wife and friend engage in private conversation), and then returns just in time to hear this:

> *Her.*   Of this make no conclusion, lest you say
>   Your queen and I are devils. Yet go on.
>   Th' offences we have made you do we'll answer,

> If you first sinned with us, and that with us
> You did continue fault, and that you slipped not
> With any but with us.

Leon.   Is he won yet?

Her.   He'll stay, my lord.

Leon.   At my request he would not. (1.2.81–87)

Leontes apparently mistakes the plural "we" (referring to both Hermione and the wife of Polixenes) for the royal "we" (referring only to Hermione). The timing is most unfortunate for the queen, but the fault lies not in her but in the potentially hazardous ambiguities in language itself. To make matters worse, the ambiguities of Hermione's spoken language are compounded by her ambiguous gestures and body language as she and Polixenes pinch fingers and paddle palms (if we can trust the report of Leontes). Like her spoken language, Hermione's actions and gestures are susceptible to multiple interpretations, and could signify not innocent play but erotic foreplay.

The infidelities of language in the play seem implicitly linked with the suspected infidelities of Hermione. As in several of Shakespeare's plays (and in Renaissance culture generally), the waywardness and slipperiness of language are often associated with waywardness in femininity—as in the equivocating language of the weird sisters in *Macbeth*, as well as in the humor of Viola and Feste in *Twelfth Night*:

Viola   . . . They that dally nicely with words may quickly
          make them wanton.

Feste   I would therefore my sister had no name, sir.

Viola   Why, man?

Feste   Why, sir, her name's a word, and to dally with that word might make my
          sister wanton. (*Twelfth Night* 3.1.14–20)

Wanton words, like wanton women, can be dallied with and made unfaithful; words can promiscuously signify various meanings at various times. Leontes misperceives Hermione as a "bed-swerver" (2.1.94) in part because words themselves are bed swervers—"cojoining" wantonly with an infinite variety of other words, hopping shamelessly from one syntactic and semantic bed to another.

In radical opposition to the refined, stable, Pentecostal language of the source text, the stage play reenacts Babel. Along with various Biblical allusions (such as the garden and the doctrine of ill doing), the play evokes the Biblical collapse of language from univocal clarity to multivocal confusion.

Beginning with the opening scene of courtly and refined dialogue between Camillo and Archidamus—reminiscent perhaps of the euphuistic style of the romance—the language of the play collapses in the depraved and grotesque ravings of Leontes.

Of course, the villain of the play is not language, precisely, but Leontes in his perverse eagerness to seize upon the most sinister interpretations that language can suggest. Other characters, such as Polixenes and Hermione, though they speak in language that is inevitably ambiguous and unruly, manage to overcome the pitfalls of gross misinterpretation by assuming interpretive limits. In conversation, they apparently assume that intended meanings are virtuous, and that any perverse suggestions are innocent or unintended. When, for instance, Polixenes reflects on his growth from boyhood into maturity, his language may very well suggest various erotic possibilities, such as vital spirits and phallic erection:

> Had we pursued that life,
> And our weak spirits ne'er been higher reared
> With stronger blood, we should have answered heaven
> Boldly "Not guilty.". . . (1.2.71–74)

Yet Hermione either overlooks such possibilities, or takes the remark as playful and humorous. In other words, Hermione retains an ability to distinguish primary texts from unruly subtexts. In Biblical terms, she enjoys the Pentecostal grace which helps compensate for the fallen imperfections of language. For Hermione and Polixenes, the indeterminacy of language (though impossible to eliminate or control) is held in check—not by any certain knowledge or verifiable proof but by mutual trust and faith.

As we see in Hermione and Polixenes, interpretations of language depend largely on assumptions and presuppositions—on faith—and Leontes has lost all faith, and thus his interpretations of words and gestures become entirely unhinged and free floating. Overwhelmed by the full and unqualified effects of Babel, Leontes seizes upon subtexts of the most sinister kind and misreads them as authoritative and reliable texts. Though he fears "barbarism" in any language that fails to distinguish between prince and beggar (2.1.85), he himself falls into a language that erases all distinctions, that reduces all meanings to the most degraded of possibilities. Taking giddy delight in the wanton multiplicities of language, he plays with various meanings of the word "play," ultimately reducing all forms of "play" to an undistinguished level of human perversity:

> Go, play, boy, play. Thy mother plays, and I
> Play too, but so disgraced a part, whose issue
> Will hiss me to my grave. (1.2.187–89)

For Leontes, the innocent and boyish "play" of Mamillius collapses into the adulterous "play" of Hermione and his own sinister "play" as he studies his wife and friend. Similarly, when Hermione proclaims

> . . . I have spoke to the purpose twice:
> The one forever earned a royal husband,
> Th' other for some while a friend (1.2.106–08),

the word "friend"—which in the early seventeenth century could mean either friend or lover (see *Measure for Measure* 1.4.29 and *OED*)—becomes for Leontes a virtual confirmation of his wife's guilt. Ironically, Leontes seems to relish the indeterminacies of language, and yet he insists that linguistic meanings can be fully determined according to his own perverse will. Of all possible interpretations, he seizes upon only the most degraded as credible: a mere "sigh" becomes "a note infallible / Of breaking honesty" (1.2.286–87). The tyrant king attempts to tyrannize over the court and over language—to force words and gestures to signify according to his will: "All's true that is mistrusted" (2.1.48). For Leontes, all evil is evil, and all good is evil in disguise.

As the king loses faith, his language becomes fallen, filthified, infected. While Iago thinks hideous thoughts and voices them coolly, Leontes speaks a language that virtually copulates with itself as word spawns word in a seamy and licentious process of linguistic fornication. His deranged language becomes a kind of lust in action: words become detached and loose, free floating, without fidelity to any fixed or single referent, and thus promiscuously and wantonly interactive:

> Too hot, too hot!
> To mingle friendship far is mingling bloods. (1.2.108–09)
>
> Inch thick, knee-deep, o'er head and ears a forked one! (186)

Leontes seems lost in the endless, wayward, obscene play of his own words, uncertain himself where the potential obscenities in language may lead him. Phrases such as "Too hot" and "Inch thick" suggest endless possibilities of meaning, and his habitually deferred and vague syntax serves only to multiply such possibilities. Lost in his own disjointed and byzantine grammar, he seems unsure where he is going, until language gets him there:

> Ha' not you seen, Camillo—
> But that's past doubt; you have, or your eyeglass
> Is thicker than a cuckold's horn—or heard—
> For to a vision so apparent, rumor
> Cannot be mute—or thought—for cogitation
> Resides not in that man that does not think—
> My wife is slippery? (1.2.266–72)

"Seen," "heard," "thought"—each word cries out in Leontes' mind for parenthetical scrutiny of its diverse and perverse implications. In the dizzying labyrinth of Leontes' illogic, even Camillo's "eyeglass" partakes of gross thickness and cuckoldry, at least in part because a sequence of linguistic connotations seems to make it so: seen, eyes, eyeglass, horn, cuckoldry. Moreover, no one in the play can keep reins on the libidinous implications of language, at least not when in the company of Leontes. Even the seemingly straightforward responses of Camillo become susceptible to gross misinterpretation:

> *Cam.* You had much ado to make his anchor hold.
> When you cast out, it still came home.
>
> *Leon.* Didst note it?
>
> *Cam.* He would not stay at your petitions, made
> His business more material.
>
> *Leon.* Didst perceive it? (1.2.212–15)

As usual there is no telling precisely what runs through Leontes' head, except to say that his mind is reeling, and that the remarks of Camillo are meaningful to Leontes in ways Camillo could never hope to guess. Leontes projects onto Camillo his own semiotic hypersensitivity: "thy conceit is soaking, will draw in / More than the common blocks" (1.2.223–24). As the exchange between the two men continues, words and phrases continue to surfeit with unruly implications:

> *Leon.* Ay, but why?
>
> *Cam.* To satisfy your Highness and the entreaties
> Of our most gracious mistress.
>
> *Leon.* Satisfy?
> Th' entreaties of your mistress? Satisfy?
> Let that suffice. (1.2.230–34)

"Satisfy" becomes a semantic vortex for all the erotic imaginings that haunt the infected mind of Leontes. All potentially virtuous meanings of "satisfy" vanish as Leontes insists that "satisfy" can only signify the satisfaction of lust (as in *Titus Andronicus* 2.3.180—"let them satisfy their lust on thee"). The most trivial and innocent words harbor latent corruption, even when talking to his young son:

> What, hast smutched thy nose?
> They say it is a copy out of mine. Come, captain,
> We must be neat; not neat, but cleanly, captain.
> And yet the steer, the heifer, and the calf
> Are all called neat. (1.2.121–25)

Like Camillo's eyeglass, the word "neat" (pertaining at first merely to a smudge on the boy's nose) comes to suggest a sequence of increasingly vile associations: neat, cattle, horns, cuckoldry.

In a parody of creation *ex nihilo*, Leontes by sheer power of the word, the logos, creates something out of nothing:

> Is this nothing?
> Why, then the world and all that's in 't is nothing,
> The covering sky is nothing, Bohemia nothing,
> My wife is nothing, nor nothing have these nothings,
> If this be nothing. (1.2.291–95)

As every spectator on and off stage realizes, this is indeed nothing. The babel of Leontes' language miscreates a fantasy founded upon airy nothing. (The very word "nothing" is repeated so often by Leontes that it is itself exhausted of meaning, reduced to nonsense.) Leontes withdraws from the world of communal faith and trust into a private fantasy fabricated upon "foundations" and a "center" that do not exist:

> If I mistake
> In those foundations which I build upon,
> The center is not big enough to bear
> A schoolboy's top. (2.1.101–04)

The very image of a "top," especially if Mamillius plays with an actual top on stage, functions as an appropriate emblem for Leontes' vertiginous and out-of-control fantasies. Alone in his suspicions, and physically distanced from all other characters on stage (habitually dismissing Mamillius, Paulina, Antigonus, the infant, and even Apollo), Leontes communes only with himself in a solipsistic and entirely self-referential nightmare of language gone haywire.

In the far more precise and stable linguistic order of the source text, possibilities of meaning are more rigidly confined, usually in antithetical pairs. As dependably as good fortune is followed by bad, virtually all dilemmas in Greene's romance are presented in an orderly scheme of neatly opposed alternatives. For instance, when King Pandosto decides to poison his friend King Egistus, he approaches his servant Franion (Camillo) with two clear options:

> he began with bitter taunts to take up his man, and to lay before him two baytes; preferment, and death: saying that if he would poyson Egistus, he should advance him to high dignities: if he refused to do it of an obstinate minde, no torture should be too great to requite his disobedience. (160)

When Franion is then left alone to consider his options, he proceeds to contemplate the various pros and cons in a well-balanced series of antitheses:

> Ah Franion, treason is loved of many, but the traitor hated of all: unjust offences may for a time escape without danger, but never without revenge. . . . [C]onscience once stayned with innocent bloud, is always tyed to a guiltie remorse. Prefer thy content before riches, and a cleare minde before dignitie; so beeing poore, thou shalt have rich peace, or else rich, thou shalt enjoy disquiet. (160–61)

Moreover, Franion systematically marshals a series of clear moral and political imperatives for Pandosto to spare the life of Egistus: "shewing him what an offence murther was to the gods," "causeles crueltie did seldome or never escape without revenge," "if he now should, without any just or manifest cause, poyson him, it would . . . be a great dishonor to his Magesty, and a meanes to sow perpetuall enmitie betweene the Sycilians and the Bohemians" (160).

In opposition to the highly structured and balanced language of Franion, Shakespeare's Camillo never reviews a series of pros and cons, never indulges in internal debate, nor does he even respond to Leontes with any sort of rational argument. Instead, after his exchange with the king gets bogged down in a hopeless quagmire of semantic cross-purposes, Camillo resorts to an entirely intuitive and unverifiable proclamation of the queen's innocence: "No, no, my lord" (1.2.298). Implicit in Camillo's silences and monosyllabic protest—his refusal to say much of anything—seems a fundamental frustration with language itself. Instead of embracing language as a solid vessel of truth, Camillo hesitates to speak at all, and when he finally does speak at length, he adopts a language of calculated duplicity, saying to Leontes that if he does not poison Polixenes then he should no longer be accounted Leontes' cupbearer (which of course he will not be after he flees with Polixenes to Bohemia). Later in the scene, when he meets Polixenes, he speaks in a language so riddling and enigmatic that Polixenes cannot even comprehend him: "Be intelligent to me" (1.2.377). Unlike his romance counterpart, Camillo seems entirely to reject any hope of rational thought or plain speaking.

In the romance, the reliability of clear rational language is rarely brought into question. Language operates in a steady and sober fashion, and all characters cling fast to the credibility of rational thought—even if, on occasion, such thoughts are entirely mistaken. When, for instance, Egistus makes a swift exit so that the "grasse should not be cut from under his feete" (162), all the Bohemians are convinced the evidence speaks against him: "the sodaine and speedie passage of Egistus, and the secret departure of Franion, induced them (the circumstances throughly considered) to thinke that both the Proclamation was true, and the king greatly injured" (163–64). Yet however mistaken the Bohemians may be on such particulars, their empirical and rational sensibilities are never quite discredited. On the contrary, the lords demonstrate a remarkably clear-sighted apprehension of the larger, transcendent schemes of providential justice. The lords sternly warn the king not to punish the infant since "causeless crueltie, nor innocent blood never scapes without revenge" (166), and indeed the tragic conclusion of the romance (Pandosto's despair and suicide) fully endorses the confident, clear-sighted rationality of the lords. In Greene's text, language and rational thought, though occasionally slipshod on particulars, prove fully in accord with ultimate truth. Though Greene's lords may be wrong in trifles, they are most right in deepest consequence. The orderly and balanced phrases they habitually articulate—"causeless cruelty, nor innocent blood never scapes without revenge"—seem inscribed in the very nature and fabric of the universe.

In Shakespeare's play, empirical evidence and rational thought never hold such sway. Even though ocular proof for Polixenes' guilt may seem evident to all—"Never / Saw I men scour so on their way. I eyed them / Even to their ships" (2.1.34–36)—Shakespeare's lords remain unconvinced. Clinging to their faith in the innocence of the queen, they apparently interpret the scouring expressions of Polixenes and Camillo as signs of fear rather than guilt. The lords in the play entirely dismiss what the king takes as firm evidence. Indeed, Antigonus responds with a thoroughly unempirical and unverifiable defense of Hermione—offering to geld his daughters and glib himself if the queen proves false. Like Camillo, Antigonus offers not a reasoned argument but rather an assertion of faith. Even the irrepressible Paulina, a woman of "boundless tongue" (2.3.92), finds her weapon of choice not in language or rational argument but in moments of strategically arranged speechlessness:

> We do not know
> How he may soften at the sight o' the child.
> The silence of pure innocence
> Persuades when speaking fails. (2.2.37–42)

Though the king responds by ordering the infant consumed with fire, he relents when the court resorts to mute gesture: "We all kneel" (2.3.153). Keeping with the spirit of anti-rationality in the play, Antigonus then takes up the infant in hope of a miracle, something beyond comprehension, indeed something, to use his wife's term, "monstrous to our human reason" (5.1.41):

> Come on, poor babe.
> Some powerful spirit instruct the kites and ravens
> To be thy nurses! (2.3.185–87)

In the source text, there are no counterparts to Antigonus or Paulina. Instead, various sailors set the infant adrift in a small boat, feeling pity for the babe but leaving her to what, rationally, they can only anticipate will be certain death.

In the source text, the supreme credibility of language and rational thought—in spite of a few minor setbacks and contradictions—is repeatedly upheld. Even the persecuted queen Bellaria continues to express firm confidence in the power of reasonable explanation and clings to a sense of language as a fully reliable vessel of truth. In her defense, she repeatedly cites "choller" (168) as the cause of the king's jealousy, fully confident that the source of his madness can be definitively known and articulated as a matter of humor imbalance. When accused in open court, Bellaria also expresses an unshaken confidence in verifiable evidence: "[she] desired that she might have Lawe and Justice, for mercy shee neyther craved nor hoped for; and that those perjured wretches, which had falsely accused her to the king, might be brought before her face, to give in evidence" (168). When the king refuses, Bellaria proceeds to the higher authority of the oracle, but with the very same confidence in a rational, fully comprehensible order in the universe, above the deceptions of malicious reports and jealous surmises:

If the devine powers bee privy to humane actions (as no doubt they are) I hope my patience shall make fortune blushe, and my unspotted life shall staine spightful discredit. For although lying Report hath sought to appeach mine honor, and Suspition hath intended to soyle my credit with infamie: yet where Vertue keepeth the Forte, Report and Suspition may assayle, but never sack: how I have led my life before Egistus comming, I appeale Pandosto to the Gods and to thy conscience. . . . and that this is true which I have heere rehearsed, I referre myself to the devine Oracle. (170–71)

The equivalent speech in the play demonstrates just how closely Shakespeare worked with Greene's text in mind—or in hand:

> Since what I am to say must be but that
> Which contradicts my accusation, and
> The testimony on my part no other
> But what comes from myself, it shall scarce boot me
> To say "not guilty." Mine integrity,
> Being counted falsehood, shall, as I express it,
> Be so received. But thus: if powers divine
> Behold our human actions, as they do,
> I doubt not then but innocence shall make
> False accusation blush and tyranny
> Tremble at patience. (3.2.22–32)

Like her counterpart, Hermione expresses firm confidence in the orderly and dependable workings of providential justice, convinced that her patience ultimately will overcome the king's tyranny. Yet quite unlike her counterpart, Hermione prefaces her defense with a sweeping disclaimer of the value of language and empirical evidence. While Bellaria desires to have her accusers brought before her so that she might counter false evidence with true, Hermione dismisses the entire process as hopelessly degraded. Like Cordelia before Lear, Hermione may end up saying much, but only after poignantly saying "nothing." Though she proceeds to marshal all the evidence she can muster, she places little weight upon such evidence. Instead, she continues to insist upon the problematic nature of language itself, rejecting the accusations of the king—"You speak a language I understand not" (3.2.80)—and even belittling the value of her own speech—"For behold me . . . here standing / To prate and talk for life and honor 'fore / Who please to come and hear" (3.2.37–42). Though she repeatedly echoes the very words of her counterpart in the romance, Hermione stresses what Bellaria never mentions, an irresolvable dissonance between divine truth and human representations of truth. Her innocence, she proclaims, eludes the representational power of a court trial: "which is more / Than history can pattern, though devised / And played to take spectators" (3.2.35–37). Moreover, like the trial, the stage play itself—devised to take spectators—is inevitably a gross misrepresentation. Unlike the source text, which aspires to full and authentic representation of the world, the stage play persistently undermines any claims to the status of pure truth.

In effect, Shakespeare seizes upon the minor lapses and inconsistencies of language and rational thought in the romance—potentially subversive ironies that the source text suppresses or overcomes—and develops such ironies into a wholesale distrust of language and rational thought in the stage play. Dismissing language as a medium of truth, Hermione's distinctive way of knowing is anti-rational—she awakens her faith (even without instructions from Paulina). While Bellaria cannot determine the innocence or guilt of Franion for lack of solid evidence—"I can neither accuse him nor excuse him, for I was not privie to his departure" (171)—Hermione intuitively affirms Camillo's innocence:

> All I know of it
> Is that Camillo was an honest man;
> And why he left your court, the gods themselves,
> Wotting no more than I, are ignorant. (3.2.73–76)

She proclaims an unverifiable faith in Camillo as he (and Antigonus) proclaimed faith in her. Thus when Hermione finally ends her defense by echoing the very words of her counterpart—"I do refer me to the oracle" (3.2.115)—she may voice the same words but she means something quite different. For Bellaria the oracle is a higher power on a hierarchical scale of rational forces; for Hermione the oracle is a force of another order entirely—transcendent, beyond rationality, outside the scope of depraved and fallen human language.

Even the oracles in the two texts, though virtually identical, suggest profoundly different assumptions about language. In the romance, the truth of the divine oracle proves fully accessible to human discernment:

> Bellaria is chast: Egistus blameless: Franion a true subject: Pandosto treacherous: his babe an innocent, and the King shal live without an heire: if that which is lost be not founde. (169)

The meaning—without cryptic or Delphic complexity—is fully transparent and available to human reason: that which is lost (the babe) will indeed be found (years later when she happens upon Pandosto's court). In the play, however, the oracle is used with teasing simplicity, but with dimensions of significance unapprehensible until Act 5. What gets found in the play is not merely Perdita, but (against all evidence to the contrary) Hermione, and (against any sense of just deserts) the innocence of Leontes, along with Camillo as surrogate Antigonus, and Florizel as new son to replace Mamillius. In Shakespeare's play, the simple and plain language of the oracle ultimately proves elusive, with an overplus of meanings that defy rational discernment. Indeed, Shakespeare's oracle is described as "ear-deaf'ning" (3.1.9), suggesting a meaningfulness beyond the scope of human perception. Ironically, the unreliability of language in the stage play turns out to be not only the disease but the cure: the slipperiness of Apollo's oracle proves a redemptive countermeasure to the slipperiness of Leontes' language in the earlier scenes.

In the fully transparent and rational world of the romance, the queen dies—and stays dead. Moreover, the cause of her death, like the cause of the king's "choller," is fully knowable and precisely explained. Bellaria dies from an early modern version of cardiac arrest: "surcharged before with extreme joy [for the oracle], and now suppressed with heavie sorrowe [for her son's sudden death], her vital spirites were so stopped, that she fell downe presently dead" (171). She dies from the effects of excessive and conflicting passions—as well as from the rigorous demands of euphuistic rhetoric as "extreme joy" cries out for its balanced antithesis in "heavie sorrowe."

Pandosto instantly repents for his misdeeds. Jolted into a suddenly clarified vision of his own guilt and the ineluctable mechanisms of providential justice, he prophetically anticipates his own death as just recompense:

> Unnaturall actions offend the Gods more than men, and causelesse crueltie never scapes without revenge. . . . Well, sith the Gods meane to prolong my dayes, to increase my dolour, I will offer my guilite bloud a sacrifice to those sackles soules, whose lives are lost by my rigorous folly. (171–72)

Though his rash suicide attempt is thwarted by the lords, providential justice works precisely as Pandosto anticipates. The gods indeed prolong his days to increase his dolour: years later he commits further infamy by attempting (unknowingly) to seduce his own daughter, and when he realizes what he has done, he falls into even greater despair, and finally succeeds in suicide. The ending of the romance is precisely the ending that Franion, the various lords, and even Pandosto anticipate: "causelesse crueltie never scapes without revenge" (see 160, 166, 171). Such prophetic accuracy attests to a firm accord between human logic and divine logic; indeed, the language of men and the designs of Providence prove virtually identical.

Shakespeare carries over the king's despair from source text to stage play, but to a radically different end. Whereas Pandosto's madness maintains a steady course toward despair, attempted suicide, more despair, and finally effective suicide, Leontes' despair leads unexpectedly and paradoxically to hope and renewal. His despair becomes the very ground of rebirth, like the "dungy earth" (2.1.158) out of which spring returns. Not that Leontes' despair is any less profound—on the contrary, Shakespeare employs Paulina (without counterpart in the romance) to intensify the king's grief, prodding him into what seems like the utter hopelessness of Pandosto:

> Do not repent these things, for they are heavier
> Than all thy woes can stir. Therefore betake thee
> To nothing but despair. A thousand knees
> Ten thousand years together, naked, fasting,
> Upon a barren mountain, and still winter
> In storm perpetual, could not move the gods
> To look that way thou wert. (3.2.208–14)

In urging despair and invoking the powers of even-handed justice, Paulina intertextually voices the rigorous and orderly designs of the source text. Like Franion and the various lords in the romance, Paulina apprehends a certain and transparent cosmic order, sure to strike the king with just retribution at some moment when he is most ripe for damnation. Yet, as we later discover, Paulina adopts the moral rigor of the romance to a quite contrary purpose, a purpose that remains hidden and unintelligible until the final act.

When we next see Paulina, sixteen years later, she apparently has not let up, still tormenting the penitent king, still keeping his sorrows "Afresh" (5.1.148), reminding Leontes of the loss of his son and daughter, the "unparallel'd" virtue of the queen, and the "just cause" Hermione must hold against him (5.1.16,61). Paulina even taunts Leontes with a vision of the ghost of Hermione returning to haunt him should he seek a new wife: "Were I the ghost that walk'd . . . I'd shriek, that even your ears / Should rift to hear me, and the words that follow'd / Should be, 'Remember mine'" (5.1.63–67). As agent of intertextuality, with one foot planted firmly in the source text, Paulina reminds Leontes (and the audience) of how a returned Hermione would act in a fully rational and just world—like that of the romance.

Yet Paulina also speaks an opposing, alternative language of mystery and paradox. In Act 3, she briefly relents from her bitter denunciation of Leontes, blatantly contradicting herself: "What's gone and what's past help / Should be past grief" (3.2.222–23). And in Act 5, she mysteriously proclaims that the king must marry and produce an heir, and yet he must not marry or produce an heir until his "lost child be found" (5.1.40), a prospect that Paulina insists is beyond all reasonable expectations: "Which that it shall / Is all as monstrous to our human reason / As my Antigonus to break his grave / And come again to me" (5.1.40–43). No one on stage, including the king, can possibly comprehend what she has up her sleeve—it all sounds like irrational nonsense, which, of course, is her point. Paulina alternates between two languages, two ethical systems, two theologies: one of rational order and justice, the other of mystery and paradox. Her name, spoken for the first time in the fifth act, begins to suggest a kinship to St. Paul—or, rather, the two opposing voices of St. Paul in the New Testament. Like her apostolic namesake, Paulina both upholds the value of the old law—as a necessary though "interim measure" of strict and precise written codes (Galatians 3:19)—while radically proposing a new law of spiritual freedom and liberation. Analogously, Paulina may suggest the two opposing identities of Saul and Paul—rigorous defender of the old law and radical proponent of the new. With the guidance of Paulina, Leontes both fulfills the demands of the old law—through sixteen years of penitence—and is liberated by the new law of grace unmerited and freely given—in the form of Hermione's return in the final scene. With a sense of paradox reminiscent of St. Paul—"The seed you sow does not come to life unless it has first died" (1 Corinthians 15:36)—Paulina guides Leontes through a death of the old self and a rebirth into a new-found innocence and purity—"having died to that which held us bound, we are released from the law, to serve God in a new way, the way of the spirit in contrast to the old way of a written code" (Romans 7:6). In her conflicting and paradoxical counsel to Leontes, Paulina fulfills her double function as both agent of the old law—to which the romance remains faithful—and agent of the new law which emerges in the conclusion of the stage play. In effect, the rigorous linguistic and moral order of Greene's romance comes to suggest the old dispensation, which the play, in the figure of Paulina, both appropriates and supersedes.[9]

Unlike Shakespeare's play, the romance ends not with paradox or miracle but with unrelenting rigor, balance, and symmetry. After sixteen years, Pandosto remains thoroughly unchanged, still plagued by bouts of excess "choller" (192). When Dorastus and Fawnia (Florizel and Perdita) arrive in Bohemia with a fabricated story of how they came from Trapalonia, King Pandosto, in a choleric and "rough reply" (192), dismisses their story as a pack of lies (which it is), and proceeds to imprison Dorastus and set his lustful eye unknowingly upon his own daughter:

> Pandosto amased at the singular perfection of Fawnia, stood halfe astonished. . . . contrarie to his aged yeares began to be somewhat tickled with the beauty of Fawnia, in so much that hee could take no rest, but cast in his old head a thousand new devises. (192–93)

After sixteen years, he persists in "unfitte fancies" (193), only this time not in the form of jealousy but in the more depraved and unnatural form of incestuous desire (thus his jealous suspicions in the beginning are euphuistically balanced by incestuous desire at the end).

Eventually, King Egistus receives word of his son's imprisonment, and sends ambassadors to urge Pandosto to free the boy and summarily execute Fawnia, Porrus (the old shepherd), and Capnio (servant of Dorastus and counterpart to Camillo). The old shepherd, in fear of his life, tries to evade execution by disavowing paternity to Fawnia. He explains how he discovered her as an infant when she drifted ashore in a small boat, and he displays the material evidence of a chain and jewels found with the child. The king, suddenly realizing the identity of his daughter, "leapt from his seate, and kissed Fawnia, wetting her tender cheeks with his teares" (198). His "newe joy" (198), however, is but a temporary reprieve before the inevitable antithesis of profound grief. After celebrating the uniting of the two kingdoms in a new-found heir, everyone travels to Sicilia for the marriage. But soon Pandosto begins to recollect his many offenses, now compounded by attempted incest, and he sinks into utter despair and this time succeeds in suicide: "moved with these desperate thoughts, he fell into a melancholie fit, and to close up a Comedie with a Tragicall stratageme, he slewe himselfe" (199). In the euphuistic order of the romance, the moment of comedy demands its antithesis in tragedy. Pandosto is slain (like his wife sixteen years earlier) by a co-conspiracy of providential order and rhetorical order, which in the romance prove virtually identical.

Shakespeare's king does not suffer the Oedipus-like fate of incest and self-mutilation doled out by the gods in the romance. Instead, unforeseen and unexpected events disrupt the forces of even-handed justice. Yet the miracle of the final scene occurs only after the play intertextually evokes the ending offered by the source text. Indeed, the incestuous desires of King Pandosto momentarily emerge in Leontes when Florizel pleads for him to act as advocate:

Flor.   . . . At your request
         My father will grant precious things as trifles.

Leon.   Would he do so, I'd beg your precious mistress,
         Which he counts but a trifle.

Paul.   Sir, my liege,
         Your eye hath too much youth in't. (5.1.221–25)

Ironically, Perdita fulfills all of the stipulations for a new wife demanded by Paulina: "Unless another, / As like Hermione as is her picture, / Affronts his eye" (5.1.73–75). The king's momentary desire for his own daughter recalls the ending of the source text, and what (in a more orderly and euphuistic world) would become of such a king as he stands on the brink of self-damning incest. Yet after intertextually veering towards the ending of the romance, the play sidesteps such an ending. Paulina quickly intervenes, and plucks Leontes back from the edge of disaster. Unlike the incestuous king of the romance, Leontes emerges as an advocate and defender of youth, leading the young couple off stage to attempt a reconciliation with the angry Polixenes. While in Act 1 Leontes could see only guilt in the innocent Hermione, he now sees only innocence in the somewhat guilty (fib-telling) Florizel and Perdita, who concoct a tale about coming from Libya. Leontes' response is a small but miraculous act of child-like faith—sixteen years of despair having done wonders for him.

A sense of wonder is evoked in the ending of the romance as well, but there it is confined to the king's reunion with his daughter, and subsequent reconciliation with Dorastus and King Egistus. In the play, these reunions are appropriated but relegated to the relatively minor status of off-stage events. The reports of the reunion by the three gentlemen in effect defer the ending of the play, intensifying our sense of wonder in that the ending we were led to expect (the reunions of the romance) turns out not to be the ending after all, but rather a prelude to the ending. Once again, the play intertextually evokes the ending of the source, only to swerve towards the unexpected.

The penultimate scene of the stage play not only wraps up the happy reunions of the romance, but also serves as a reminder of the problematic nature of language throughout the play. The three gentlemen who report the reunions repeatedly express profound frustrations with language. Each gentleman has gleaned only a piece of the story, and though their various accounts do not contradict, their reports do not add up to the full authentic story, which they repeatedly insist is beyond verbal representation: "cannot be spoken of," "lames report," "undoes description," "ballad-makers cannot be able to express it," "so like an old tale the verity of it is in strong suspicion" (5.2.25–59). Moreover, the three gentlemen describe characters who seem to have given up on spoken language altogether, only to commune in silent gesture: "speech in their dumbness, language in their very gesture," "casting up of eyes, holding up of hands, with contenance of such distraction" (5.2.14–15, 47–49). The three eyewitnesses can only offer piecemeal and disjointed accounts of events that seem to defy spoken language altogether. As one of the gentlemen aptly remarks, he can offer only "a broken delivery of the business" (5.2.10–11)—indeed "broken" in several Renaissance senses of the word: spoken pantingly and out of breath (all speech is "eyr ybroken" as Chaucer says), spoken with imperfect syntax, and spoken in incomplete and disjointed fragments (see *OED*). The phrase recalls the many instances of "broken" language in the stage play: Leontes' disjointed speeches about Hermione, the Clown's inept report of Antigonus' death, Autolycus' nonsense ballads. All language, indeed the play itself, is a "broken delivery," an impossible attempt to convey the full truth of experience. Verbal representations, as the three gentlemen repeatedly confess and the play implicitly confirms, are inevitably and invariably misrepresentations.

The concluding scene of the stage play supersedes not only the happy reunions narrated in the source but also the elegant and deterministic language that continually characterizes the romance. Even more, the final scene moves towards a rejection of language itself, and an attempt to communicate beyond language—or at least beyond spoken language. The play moves from the broken though verbose language of the three gentlemen, to the short and plain diction of Leontes, and finally to long pauses of gesture and pure silence. On a larger scale, the play develops from the babel of Leontes in the first three acts, to the more simple though often inept language of the Bohemian shepherds, to the nonlanguage of the final scene.[10]

Leontes' fall into a labyrinth of unstable language proves, after sixteen years of penance, a fortunate fall—a dissolution of his old self—from which he emerges with a newly awakened aptitude for the nonverbal and nonrational (not unlike Pericles who recovers his daughter only after three months of pure silence). Initiated into the paradoxes of Pauline theology, Leontes comes to distrust the world of "settled senses" (5.3.72), and emerges with a budding faith in the unseen, the unverifiable, the unspeakable. While earlier in the play Leontes lived up to the implications of his name by tyrannizing lion-like over everyone, in the final scene he barely moves or speaks without instructions from Paulina. Indeed, the "feminine" (silent, chaste, obedient) Leontes seems entirely under the spell of the "masculine" Paulina as she controls and modulates his every action and reaction, guiding him into moments of silence—"I like your silence; it the more shows off / Your wonder"—to brief moments of speech—"But yet speak; first you, my liege"—and back to pure silence and stillness—"It is required / You do awake your faith; then, all stand still" (21–22, 94–95). Only after Leontes promises that "No foot shall stir" (98) does Paulina awaken the statue, and from that moment until Leontes' closing speech in the play, he speaks only once, and even then his language is simple, concrete, almost entirely monosyllabic: "O, she's warm! / If this be magic, let it be an art / Lawful as eating (109–11). The text indicates virtually no physical movement by Leontes:

Paulina describes him as "transported" (69), and he is apparently so immobilized that Paulina must instruct him not to "shun" Hermione but to present his hand to her (105–07).[11]

Much of the final scene is composed of barely interrupted silences—long pauses of astonishment and wonder. The sparse, minimalist language, almost bare of imagery, seems little more than background commentary to the more prominent language of silent gesture, as Perdita kneels before the statue, and Leontes undergoes a reverse metamorphosis from flesh to stone—wishing to remain so "twenty years together" (71).[12] At the focal point of these silent gestures stands a painted statue accompanied by music—sculpture, painting, music—all distinctly nonverbal arts. In theatrical performances, the silent statue almost inevitably becomes the primary, if not exclusive, focus of the audience's attention, especially for audience members new to the play (who are trying to figure out if what they see on stage is meant to be a statue of Hermione or Hermione pretending to be a statue). Indeed, at the climactic moment of the play the audience becomes far more attentive to the visual presence of the statue than to what is being said about the statue.

The silent tableau of all the characters on stage (and all the audience members off stage) fixed in wonder on the life-like statue of Hermione presents what seems a supreme transcendent moment. In the pure nonlanguage of silent gesture, all the tensions and discordant forces in the play converge in a final totalizing vision. Though the three gentlemen had complained earlier about the irreconcilability of language and experience, representations and truth, art and nature, all such tensions now seem dissolved. In the final moments of the play, art (the statue) not only represents nature but is identical with nature: the statue of Hermione is indeed the living Hermione. At the moment the statue animates with life, all borders between nature and art seem erased. Likewise, the correlative tensions between time and timelessness seem dissolved: Hermione stands before us as aged and wrinkled queen but also as her youthful self in the form of Perdita, Leontes appears as old man but also as boy eternal in Florizel, Mamillius is dead and rotten and yet returned in the new son-in-law (born the very same month), and even Antigonus (though he has gone a progress through the guts of a bear) returns in the figure of Camillo (a new husband for Paulina). The moment presents a shimmering double vision of both the still point of timelessness and the turning world of time. Even the audience members (nature) and the actors (art) fuse in a moment of shared surprise—the only instance in all thirty-seven plays when a vital secret has been kept from the audience, and thus the off-stage audience and the on-stage actors converge in a moment of wonder and suspense. Moreover, the forces of art and nature fuse as we see the statue— the artificial creation of Julio Romano—juxtaposed to Perdita—the natural creation of her mother Hermione. Even more, this climactic and totalizing synthesis of art in nature, timelessness in time, eternity in mutability, is augmented by a masterstroke of pagan-Christian syncretism: Hermione as Proserpina/Christ stirs to life in a pagan/Christian chapel, miraculously returning from the Ovidian/Biblical world of the dead. The play absorbs and embraces both a pagan view of immortality (achieved through regeneration) and a Christian view of immortality (achieved through resurrection). In effect, the primary theme of Greene's romance, announced in the subtitle, "The Triumph of Time," is both appropriated and superseded as the play offers a double vision of the triumph of time and the triumph of timelessness over time.

Shakespeare's multilayered synthesis of opposing concepts, especially art and nature, stands in radical contrast to the consistently well ordered and precise linguistic categories of Greene's romance. In the romance, art and nature never converge but remain in stable euphuistic opposition. When, for instance, Dorastus comes to woo Fawnia not in the garb of his princely self but artificially disguised as a shepherd, she playfully teases him, saying that art and nature cannot so easily be tampered with:

> all that weare Cooles are not Monkes: painted Eagles are pictures, not Eagles.
> Zeusis Grapes were like Grapes, yet shadowes: rich clothing make not
> princes: nor homely attyre beggers. (185)

As usual in the romance, concepts fall snugly and firmly into place: an eagle is one thing, a painted eagle quite another. Nature and art remain rationally distinct with borders boldly intact.

Shakespeare's text, however, problematizes the art-nature dichotomy. Polixenes expounds on how all art is created within and indirectly by nature, which evokes the medieval commonplace that all nature is God's art. Moreover, at that very moment in the play, Polixenes offers his advice to a Perdita who is both artificial Queen of the Feast and (unknown to herself) natural-born royalty. Such moments in the play tease us out of thought, exposing common linguistic formulations as inadequate to contain the dizzying flux of experience. The play continually emphasizes transformations, mutations, Ovidian metamorphoses, not only of the statue into Hermione, but of prince into shepherd, shepherdess into princess, tyrant into penitent, cutpurse into agent of providential designs, shepherd and son into gentlemen. Even incidental phrases such as "summer's death" and "birth / Of trembling winter" (4.4.80–81) tend to confound opposing concepts of birth and death. In contrast to the rhetorical and semantic stabilities of the source text, language in the play seems continually fluid and slippery, always on the move. Binary oppositions refuse to step in line, betraying the inevitable falsifications and misrepresentations in all textual and linguistic constructs.

Even the profound differences between Leontes' madness in Act 1 and his faith in Act 5 seem precariously on the verge of a breakdown. The very terms are used interchangeably: as his jealous madness was called "faith" in Act 1.2.429, his faith is called "madness" in Act 5.3.73. Though Paulina insists that the faith she calls upon must not be mistaken for "wicked powers," "unlawful business," or a "spell" (5.3.91, 96, 105), her anxious and repeated denials suggest a potential intimacy and kinship between mystical faith and deluded madness. Though Leontes' faith in the final scene evolves not in the slipperiness of language but in mystical silence—not in solipsistic isolation but in the confirming presence of a host of fellow witnesses (nearly every character in the play shows up for the final scene)—nevertheless, both faith and madness demand a similar, and potentially disastrous, willingness to believe in things unseen, things "monstrous to our human reason" (5.1.41).[13]

Yet after thoroughly confounding the precise linguistic formulations of the source text, Shakespeare's play ironically turns against itself. In the very intoxication of the final scene—just as the play aspires to a totalizing synthesis of art and nature, time and eternity, Christianity and pagan mythology—the play stubbornly resists final closure, exposing even the reformed language and nonlanguage of the final scene as wayward and deceptive. The moment the statue becomes Hermione—just as a painted eagle becomes an eagle—Paulina intrudes upon the effects of her own spellbinding magic by telling us:

> That she is living,
> Were it but told you, should be hooted at
> Like an old tale. (5.3.115–17)

Paulina betrays the artificial stratagem of the transcendent moment, exposing the play's kinship with ludicrous old tales and fantastic ballads. She implicitly links the return of Hermione with the many contrivances that abound in the play—the bear, the figure of Time, the precisely timed sea-sickness of Perdita. Indeed, in such moments of flaunted artificiality, the play becomes even more artificial than the artifices of Greene's romance.

The play spontaneously self-deconstructs even in the very climax of its finest construction. After we are compelled to experience the resurrection of Hermione as a miracle, we are informed that the miracle was contrived—Hermione had been "preserv'd" (127). The statue turned flesh is revealed as a stage trick masterminded by Paulina as on-stage playwright and director. Just as the play begins to aspire to a grand unified vision—a pure mimesis that supersedes and outperforms all the elegant symmetries of the source text—the play sabotages itself, exposing its own status as an artifice, a fake, an empty sign, an assemblage of devices from old tales. With a textual skepticism akin to Montaigne—"there are more books about books than about any other subject: we do nothing but write glosses about each other" ("Of Experience" 818)—Shakespeare in effect acknowledges his text as merely a composite of texts, a literary fabrication concocted from other literary fabrications. Just as the play aspires to a totalizing synthesis akin to the romance, it denies its own claim to a pure and transcendent mimesis—a painted eagle turns out, after all, to be merely a painted eagle.

Try as it may, the final scene of the play cannot escape from the taint of language. As Paulina can arrange moments of pure silence only by giving instructions in speech, and Leontes must express his stone-like silence by verbally likening himself to stone, the climactic return of Hermione is authenticated by her ability to speak: "If she pertain to life, let her speak too" (113). As with the three gentlemen who resort to language in order to discredit language, the play cannot disentangle itself from words. The final scene may point beyond language, but simultaneously points to itself pointing. The scene may suggest truth beyond words, but acknowledges its inevitable involvement in the mistruth of words. Even the nonlanguage of silent gesture in the final scene is not free from the taint of language since (as we saw in Act 1) even gestures remain imprecise signifiers, vulnerable to wayward and unruly misinterpretations. While the source text continually upholds language as a fully reliable medium of truth, Shakespeare's revisionary text involves a more complex double strategy of exploiting language to convey truth while exposing language as a medium of mistruth. Like her apostolic namesake, Paulina directs us to look into the glass while reminding us the glass is dark and distorted.

If, by any chance, Paulina should fail to undermine the totalizing truth claims of her carefully orchestrated final scene, Autolycus serves as backup. Like Paulina, Autolycus is without counterpart in the romance, and though he speaks not one word in the final scene, as a professional hawker of ballads and old tales, he serves as a visible reminder of the propensity of language—ballads and stage plays alike—to distort, misrepresent, and contrive false truths out of airy nothing. Whether or not Autolycus keeps up his old antics by picking pockets and cutting purses, his very presence works to dispel the transcendent effects of the final scene. And yet Autolycus arrives at Paulina's gallery not alone but in the company of the old shepherd and his son, who likewise speak not one word but nevertheless silently contribute to the complexity of the ending. Perhaps in contrast to a skeptical Autolycus, they respond to the return of Hermione with rapture and innocent belief, convinced they have witnessed a wondrous miracle of stone turned flesh. Thus, even in the silent reactions of Autolycus and the shepherds, the stage play involves a double strategy of both endorsing and discrediting its own effects.[14]

In opposition to the source text, and virtually all Renaissance treatises on poetics, Shakespeare denies the mimetic claims of his art, exposing not only intricate and complex rhetoric as misrepresentation but even the more concealed rhetoric of plain speaking and silent gesture. The final scene of the play, however rapturous and enthralling (for both on-stage and off-stage audiences), remains inescapably infected with the slipperiness and infidelities of language and stage representation. Shakespeare, Paulina, and Autolycus—playwright, on-stage director, and pickpocket—converge as masters of deception and sleight of hand. In all its complexity and ingenuity, the art of the play may manage to represent "Great creating nature," but only as well as Autolycus' ballads represent whatever did happen to that woman turned into a cold fish.

Notes

1. See, for example, Smith 317–27; McDonald 315–29; and Orgel 431–37. Smith examines the high frequency of neologisms and obscure, polysyllabic, Latinate words in the speeches of Leontes in the first three acts. McDonald studies the structural complexities in the language of Leontes, his habitually digressive and circumlocutious speech in which "verbs may lag behind their subjects by several lines, and often long sentences refuse to yield up their meanings until the last possible moment" (319). Orgel argues that the language of *The Winter's Tale*, like many instances of Renaissance literary and political discourse, is often deliberately incomprehensible. Other studies that focus on the problems of language in the play include Neely 321–38; Laird 25–43; and Felperin, "Deconstruction of Presence" 3–18.

2. Though Harold Bloom excludes pre-Miltonic literature from what he calls the "anxiety of influence," (*Anxiety* 11–14), I would argue that Shakespeare's play can be read as a radical "misreading" and "misprision" of his source text. For studies of Shakespeare's use of Greene's romance, see Lawlor 96–113; Bullough 8: 115–55; Frey 50–67; and Ewbank, "From Narrative to Dramatic Language" 29–47. Except for the article by Ewbank, none of these source studies approaches the play or romance with an emphasis on the problems of language.

3. Vives called such pure words "true apellations." For the views of Agrippa, Vives; and other early humanists, see Donawerth 4, 25–31.

4. Such Renaissance humanists were following Aristotle's claim that metaphors "give names to things that have none" (qtd. in Donawerth 117).

5. With a similar linguistic skepticism, Francis Bacon remarks that "although we think we govern our words . . . yet certain it is that words, as a Tartar's bow, do shoot back upon the understanding of the wisest, and mightily entangle and pervert the judgment" (*Advancement* 134).

6. For studies of sixteenth- and seventeenth-century views of language, see Donawerth; DeGrazia; and Foucault, *The Order of Things*. Foucault examines the history of epistemological changes, arguing that in the sixteenth century language was regarded as organically linked to the world—words and things were connected by "solid and secret bonds of resemblance or affinity" (58)—while in the seventeenth century, "the peculiar existence and ancient solidity of language as a thing inscribed in the fabric of the world were dissolved in the functioning of representation; all language had value only as discourse" (43). Similarly, DeGrazia argues from a Biblical and theological perspective that in the sixteenth century language was generally regarded as a reliable medium of truth. Though language was considered to have lost its pristine condition after Babel, the deficiencies in language had been largely overcome by the gift of tongues at Pentecost, and thus corruption in language was understood to issue not from any innate depravity in language but rather from the moral corruption of the individual speaker or writer. In the seventeenth century, according to DeGrazia, a new view began to emerge which claimed that corruption was inherent in the very nature of language itself. Contrary to my argument, however, DeGrazia concludes that this later view of language was generally unavailable to Shakespeare, and that all of Shakespeare's works fall in line with more traditional views of language. Likewise, Donawerth, after surveying the views of Renaissance humanists, philosophers, and scientists, concludes that the implicit views of language in Shakespeare's plays are traditional, and that language itself is never a central concern.

7. Greene does occasionally qualify the mimetic claims of his narrative by reminding his readers that the characters spoke not the precise words of the text but rather "such like words." Yet even though Greene acknowledges that his text falls short in representing the particularities of colloquial speech, his refined and elegant discourse proves fully in accord with more significant, transcendent patterns of providential designs. Thus, if Greene's text lapses in fidelity to existence, it more than compensates in fidelity to essence.

8. For an interpretation of the speech in terms of the discourse of Renaissance medicine, see Ward 545–54. Stephen Orgel cites this speech as evidence that the language of the play is often deliberately vague, confusing, and even incomprehensible, not only for us but for Renaissance audiences as well (431–37). My argument is that the babel of Leontes' speech suffers not from lack of meaning but from unruly and uncontrolled excesses of meaning.

9. Paulina's insistence that Leontes must continue to believe that he will recover his child and gain an heir (in spite of all evidence to the contrary) may even suggest St. Paul's key example of Christian-like faith in the pre-Christian era: Abraham who continued to believe he would produce an heir in spite of his own

advanced age and the deadness of Sarah's womb—"When hope seemed hopeless, his faith was such that he became 'father of many nations,' in fulfillment of the promise, 'So shall your descendants be' " (Romans 4:18). An analogy between Paulina and Paul is mentioned by G. Wilson Knight (127), but Knight takes up the analogy only briefly, and does not explore any possible connections between Paulina and the multiple voices of Paul in the New Testament.

The strong appeal in Shakespeare's play to "faith" may carry various political implications as well. In dramatizing providential forces that are incomprehensible and yet ultimately benign, the play may imply that all providential powers, such as those of King James I, are likewise beyond ordinary human comprehension and yet immeasurably good—and thus must be fully accepted on the basis of faith. Yet the powers of King James also may be suggested in the tyrant figure of Leontes, a king whose power and willfulness are opposed on the basis of faith. The political subtexts of the play (though not the concern of this essay) seem multiple and various. Indeed, for a professional playwright under the reign of an authoritarian monarch, vague politics may have been the best politics.

10. The shift in the play from complex rhetoric to a more simple language may suggest Augustine's rejection of the intricacies of classical rhetoric in favor of the simple, yet ironically profound, language of scripture (see *Confessions* 58–60).

11. Leontes' immobilization may suggest a moment of profound unworthiness, guilt and despair—like that of King Pandosto. Thus when Hermione reaches out to embrace Leontes, she in effect frees him from his own potentially disastrous guilt.

12. As Inga-Stina Ewbank comments, "Characters' reactions to the statue are patterned in a fashion which approaches ritual. An unusual number of speeches are devoted just to underlining the emotions and postures of people on stage" ("The Triumph of Time" 97).

13. As Howard Felperin comments, Leontes' jealousy is "not the absence, but the dark side of his faith" ("Deconstruction of Presence" 16).

14. Moments of self-deconstruction may be evident in *Pandosto* as well, particularly when the refined and symmetrical prose of the narrative seems to risk toppling over from its own rhetorical weight, exposing itself as a purely linguistic construct without reference to any truth beyond its own sophisticated language. In refashioning the romance, Shakespeare may have seized upon such implications, developing and expanding them in the play. The relatively moderate style of Greene's euphuistic prose, however, does not suggest any conscious attempt at self-parody, at least not like the supremely self-conscious and self-parodying style of Lyly's *Euphues*. As Carol Thomas Neely remarks, *Pandosto* is written not so much in the euphuistic style of Lyly but more in the moderate "arcadian" style of Sidney (see Neely 321–22).

CHAPTER 6

Source Texts and Contexts

Shakespeare wrote for his age and not for all time. Indeed, in recent years we have become increasingly aware of Shakespeare's skewed, distorted, culturally conditioned representations of the world. In relation to the likely demographics of early modern England, Shakespeare's plays grossly underrepresent the underclasses and women, while grossly overrepresenting the upper classes and men. Moreover, it is highly unlikely that people in Renaissance England (even rich people) ever made a habit of speaking in blank verse, or of ending conversations with a rhymed couplet, or of making frequent use of classical allusions, neologisms, clever puns, and inventive metaphors. Rather than dramatizing life as actually lived by ordinary folk, Shakespeare favored despondent princes, ambitious Scots, foolish old kings, wife-killing Moors, and comic women who dressed up as boys and married well. The lived experiences of the vast majority of Shakespeare's contemporaries passed by without stage representation. Shakespeare is not the poet of common and ordinary human experience—indeed, that is just what he avoids. Though Shakespeare may have used Moors and cross-dressing women to explore states of mind and feeling that were indeed common in his age and that reflected and even shaped the experiences of his audience members, nevertheless we cannot deny that Shakespeare's plays are primarily the products of culturally conditioned artifice.

If one of the aims of current literary research is to dispel the notion that texts can ever transcend contexts or gain freedom from the residues of history and culture, close study of Shakespeare's sources can serve as one means to reconstitute the cultural embeddedness of Shakespeare's plays. No

doubt such a task is immensely difficult, not only because of the complexities and historical distance of Renaissance culture, but because Shakespeare's plays (unlike most Renaissance texts) have become so culturally
familiar. As the cultural heirs of Shakespeare's enormous literary influence,
our very perceptions have been shaped by his representations of human experience. Most of Shakespeare's sources, however, have not become so familiar or so naturalized. Other than specialists, few people read Lodge,
Greene, Gower, or the anonymous *Leir* play with great relish and delight.
Such texts have retained their cultural otherness—which is precisely their
value. Such clearly foreign and artificial texts (texts that Shakespeare certainly found interesting or intriguing) can serve as critical lenses through
which we can more readily discern the historical embeddedness of Shakespeare's plays—their intimacy and connectedness with the distinct concerns
of early modern England (concerns that may anticipate but are never quite
identical to our concerns). Perhaps we would come to a keener apprehension
of the peculiarities of English Renaissance culture by reading Lodge rather
than Shakespeare, yet we can also read Lodge as a *pre-text* to Shakespeare, a
textual lens through which we can reapproach Shakespeare and see his
plays not as unmediated expressions of human nature but as cultural artifices
built upon other cultural artifices.

The sources can help us expose not only the cultural embeddedness of
Shakespeare's plays, but also, and perhaps more important, the moments
when Shakespeare expands beyond the perceptual limits of his culture. In
other words, the sources can help us see not only the continuities but the dis-
continuities between Shakespeare and his contexts, the moments of textual
innovation when Shakespeare exploits his source texts in order to improvise
new dimensions and new strata of texts, which in varying degrees resist or
transgress the normative parameters of his culture.

As a general pattern, Shakespeare's strategies for rewriting his sources
seem to involve not so much revisionary developments in a more radical or a
more traditional direction, but rather revisionary developments in multiple directions. The pattern seems particularly clear in a play not discussed in this
book, *Othello*—based on a brief prose narrative in Cinthio's *Hecatommithi*.
In Cinthio, the Moor (never given a name) is described at various times by the
narrator, the ensign, and Disdemona as a hot-tempered, barbarian foreigner,
prone to extreme sexual appetite. But the Moor of the source text is also described by the narrator and Disdemona as eminently brave, virtuous, of merry
disposition, capable of extreme devotion, and possessing a mighty spirit. In
the play, Shakespeare appropriates and develops not one view over the other,
but both views more fully. In the opening scene, for instance, Iago describes

the Moor in degraded and bestial terms that far exceed anything we find in the source, while in the following scene (when we first see Othello) he appears supremely rational, cool-tempered, and self-controlled—indeed, far more so than his Moorish counterpart. Such views are then troubled, deconstructed, and reconstructed throughout the rest of the play. In effect, Shakespeare writes both with and against his source, exploiting suggestions and implications already in the source text, while improvising new dimensions of text. Similarly, in *As You Like It* Shakespeare appropriates the traditional gender types found in the source, but also develops contrary versions of gender that may be implied but remain latent and underdeveloped in the source. In *King Lear* Shakespeare refashions the old *Leir* into a play that is both more radically reformational as well as more reactionary and traditional. In response to Gower's *Confessio*, Shakespeare in *Pericles* both demotes and promotes the role of the author and the authority of the author over the text. While Greene's *Pandosto* upholds the reliability and pristine clarity of language, Shakespeare in *The Winter's Tale* demolishes the stability of language in the opening scenes, reconstitutes a more concrete language in Bohemia, and then undermines language altogether in the final scene of the play. Consistently, Shakespeare develops not merely new modes of perception, but multiple modes of perception. Working within the limits and constraints of his source texts and cultural contexts, Shakespeare demonstrates a slippery ability to move in a few directions at once, creating multiple dimensions of text within the same text—although, as revisionist, Shakespeare always enjoyed an edge, starting with rich and highly suggestive material, and reworking it into richer and more suggestive material.

Shakespeare's unrivaled textual complexity (in relation to his sources and fellow playwrights) may have served various artistic and economic interests. Textually subtle and dense plays could more adequately reflect and respond to the various tensions within English Renaissance culture: tensions between conflicting views on religion, language, gender, and authorial authority, as well as the interrelated tensions between old and new cosmologies, lingering scholasticism and emerging scientific empiricism, feudalism and capitalism, rural culture and urban culture, and so forth. I suspect that Shakespeare's plays appealed to a considerably wide range of tastes (since spectators could in effect interpretively customize each play according to individual inclinations). Furthermore, the textual density of Shakespeare's plays may have encouraged repeat customers, who would return again and again to see plays that could sustain interest over multiple viewings, thus maximizing profits for the owners of the theater company (including Shakespeare who owned ten percent of the shares).

The source texts can also function as aides in assessing or approximating the range of preconceptions that Shakespeare's audiences—never blank slates—brought with them to the theater. Like all expressions of language, texts are meaningful and comprehensible only in relation to the various assumptions and expectations of the target audience. Outside of contexts, possibilities of interpretation proliferate infinitely. Indeed, contemporary literary deconstuction thrives in a world in which texts float freely in a global marketplace, severed from any local audience with shared knowledge, experiences, and assumptions. The original settings for Shakespeare's plays, however, were not (despite the ambitious name of his theater) global in any modern sense. Though we are familiar with audiences of wide-ranging social, ethnic, racial, and national diversity, Shakespeare's theater drew an almost exclusively local crowd, audiences that by modern standards would be considered virtually monocultural. Their views were most likely as provincial and as constrained as Shakespeare's—and probably more so. Not that the views of Renaissance audience members were ever singular or homogeneous—indeed, there never was an Elizabethan world picture, but always multiple and competing pictures. Elizabethan views on religion alone could be explosively divisive and contentious. Nevertheless, such conflicting views were usually contained within relatively narrow limits. Moreover, in the open, daylight atmosphere of the Globe theater, Shakespeare's audiences would have responded to plays not merely as individuals but as a community (or mob). While modern audiences sit in the isolating privacy of darkened theaters, Shakespeare's audiences would have been constantly aware of the presence and reactions of fellow audience members who were as visible (and perhaps as audible) as the characters on stage. In writing stage plays for audiences of his contemporary Londoners to be performed in open-air theaters, Shakespeare (more than any modern playwright) could know his audiences and could work within (and against) their common assumptions and common bones of contention.

No particular source text can offer a full or precise sense of the various preconceptions of Shakespeare's audiences, but such texts (especially the longer and more complex ones) can at least suggest a significant range of such preconceptions. When crowds went to see *As You Like It*, they were well aware of various traditional views of gender, but they also knew that a woman held the throne of England and that in the city of London women enjoyed a wide range of social freedoms. Whether audience members had read Lodge's *Rosalynde* or not, their preconceptions about gender are at least partly available to us in the primary source text, a text that presents gender not from a singular perspective, but from a range of perspectives, most (but not all) of them traditional. Shakespeare's *King Lear* was acted before audiences whose views on religion were shaped by ongoing tensions between traditional and reformational Christianity—tensions that can be discerned in *The True Chronicle Historie of King Leir*, a play with strong reformational tendencies but also with lingering vestiges of medieval and Catholic Christianity. Such source texts (themselves products of intertextuality) offer not singular or univocal expressions of Renaissance culture, but multivocal expressions of conflicting tendencies within that culture. Though we can never fully know the psychological or material conditions of life in Shakespeare's London, close attention to the primary sources can provide one means by which we can glimpse the preconceptual frameworks through which Shakespeare's audiences saw and responded to his plays.

I will end with a final, though not unrelated, observation. Harold Bloom (perhaps the most influential contemporary theorist of influence) describes literary influence as an anxiety-ridden competition among great poets—a literary psychomachia. According to Bloom, young writers, confronted with the monumental achievements of the past, feel an anxious need to overcome such works which threaten to overcome and extinguish their own attempts at poetic greatness. Thus young poets "misread" their precursor texts, and attempt to rewrite such texts in new modes that surpass the poetic visions of their predecessors (see *Anxiety* 19–45). Bloom claims, however, that pre-Enlightenment writers such as Shakespeare felt little anxiety—for them the great works of the past were to be treasured as sources of benign influence. Bloom describes Shakespeare, therefore, not in anxious competition with his predecessors but as an exceptionally strong poet who readily absorbed and surpassed his literary precursors. According to Bloom, "Marlowe was swallowed up by Shakespeare, as a minnow by a whale"; when we read Shakespeare, "we confront a poetic strength that surpasses even the Yahwist, Homer, Dante, and Chaucer" (*Ruin the Sacred Truths* 53).

While Bloom situates Shakespeare within a tradition of great works, I would emphasize Shakespeare's indebtedness to assorted minor texts, such as the ones considered in this book. While Dante looked to Virgil, and Virgil looked to Homer, Shakespeare looked more often than anywhere else to Holinshed (a major source for all ten history plays, as well as for *Macbeth* and *Cymbeline*, and a minor source for *King Lear*). I would not deny the profound influence of Marlowe, Chaucer, and the Bible on Shakespeare, but such influences are submersed and dispersed throughout Shakespeare's work. When it came to the nitty-gritty business of finding materials from which to craft plays, Shakespeare operated outside any canon of great masters, resorting most often to a wide variety of minor texts. Though in *Troilus and Cressida* Shakespeare drew from Chaucer's *Troilus and Criseyde* as well as Homer's *Iliad* (in Chapman's translation), he also drew from Caxton, Lydgate, and Henryson—figures that have never and will never gain membership into any version of a literary canon. Yet even though Shakespeare competed with small fish in a small pond, I still find that Bloom's notion of literary anxiety has some bearing on the pre-Enlightenment Shakespeare. Shakespeare may not have felt particularly intimidated by his sources, but his revisionary practices do suggest a tendency to willfully and anxiously "misread" his precursor texts—to write the text the precursor writer attempted but could not achieve. Indeed, Shakespeare habitually seems to read and misread, write with and write against the textual grain of his sources. In refashioning his source materials, Shakespeare consistently seems compelled to outperform and overmaster the very texts that enabled and provided the basis for his own literary mastery.

Moreover, throughout his career in the theater business, Shakespeare never outgrew his dependency on sources, never evolved from what might be considered an apprentice stage of reworking the works of others. Shakespeare's penultimate play, *The Tempest*, may have been an especially imaginative piece of work, based very loosely upon various accounts of the New World, but his early play, *Midsummer Night's Dream*, seems equally imaginative and likewise based indirectly on a variety of sources, none of them very close to the play. More typically, Shakespeare relied extensively on prewritten texts, and most of his plays (including such late works as *Pericles*, *Cymbeline*, *The Winter's Tale*, and *Henry VIII*) are heavily indebted to primary sources. By mid and late career, Shakespeare may have written plays with more refined and controlled nuances of language and character, but his dependency on sources never diminished. As a professional playwright, under pressure to produce a steady stream of new works (thirty-seven plays in under twenty-five years), Shakespeare continued to depend heavily on prefabricated texts. Throughout his career, his creative strategies remained distinctly reactive in that his plays evolved not in some rarefied imaginative isolation but in reaction to his source texts. Shakespeare was neither a pure inventor nor a mere craftsman—but an especially able and talented improvisor. His greatest and most persistent professional skill was in reimagining the texts of other writers.

Works Cited

Adelman, Janet. "Male Bonding in Shakespeare's Comedies." *Shakespeare's "Rough Magic."* Ed. Peter Erickson and Coppelia Kahn. Newark: U of Delaware P, 1985. 73–103.

Aquinas, St. Thomas. *Compendium of Theology*. Trans. Cyril Vollert, S. J., S.T.D. St. Louis: Herder, 1947.

Augustine. *Confessions*. Trans. R. S. Pine-Coffin. New York: Penguin, 1961.

Bacon, Francis. *Advancement of Learning*. London: Dent, 1973.

Bacon, Francis. "Of Adversity." *Francis Bacon: A Selection of His Works*. Ed. Sidney Warhaft. New York: Odyssey Press, 1965. 56–57.

Barber, C. L. *Shakespeare's Festive Comedy*. Princeton: Princeton UP, 1959.

Barber, C. L., and Richard Wheeler. *The Whole Journey: Shakespeare's Power of Development*. Berkeley: U of California P, 1986.

Barthes, Roland. "The Death of the Author." *Image-Music-Text*. Trans. Stephen Heath. New York: Noonday Press, 1977. 142–48.

Beckman, Margaret. "The Figure of Rosalind in *As You Like It*." *Shakespeare Quarterly* 29 (1978): 44–51.

Belsey, Catherine. "Disrupting Sexual Difference: Meaning and Gender in the Comedies." *Alternative Shakespeares*. Ed. John Drakakis. London: Methuen, 1985. 166–90.

Berry, Edward I. "Rosalynde and Rosalind." *Shakespeare Quarterly* 29 (1978): 44–51.

Bible (*Oxford Study Bible*). Ed. M. Jack Suggs, et al. Oxford: Oxford UP, 1992.

Bloom, Harold. *The Anxiety of Influence*. Oxford: Oxford UP, 1973.

Bloom, Harold. *Ruin the Sacred Truths*. Cambridge: Harvard UP, 1987.

Briggs, Julia. *This Stage-Play World*. Oxford: Oxford UP, 1983.

Bullough, Geoffrey, ed. *Narrative and Dramatic Sources of Shakespeare*. 8 vols. London: Routledge, 1957–1975.

Calderwood, James L. "Creative Uncreation in *King Lear*." *Shakespeare Quarterly* 37 (1986): 5–19.

Calvin, John. *Institutes of the Christian Religion*. Trans. Ford Lewis Battles. 2 vols. Philadelphia: Westminster P, 1960.

Canons and Decrees of the Council of Trent. Trans. H. J. Schroeder. St. Louis: Herder, 1941.

Castiglione, Baldesar. *Book of the Courtier.* Trans. George Bull. New York: Penguin, 1967.

Cressy, David, and Lori Anne Ferrell, eds. *Religion and Society in Early Modern England: A Sourcebook.* London: Routledge, 1996.

DeGrazia, Margreta. "Shakespeare's View of Language: An Historical Perspective." *Shakespeare Quarterly* 29 (1978): 374–88.

Dollimore, Jonathan. *Radical Tragedy.* Chicago: U of Chicago P, 1984.

Donawerth, Jane. *Shakespeare and the Sixteenth-Century Study of Language.* Urbana: U of Illinois P, 1984.

Donne, John. "Meditation XVII." *Complete Poetry and Selected Prose of John Donne.* Ed. Charles M. Coffin. New York: Modern Library, 1952. 440–41.

Duffy, Eamon. *The Stripping of the Altars.* New Haven: Yale UP, 1992.

Dunbar, Mary Judith. "'To the Judgement of Your Eye': Iconography and the Theatrical Art of *Pericles.*" *Shakespeare, Man of the Theater.* Ed. Kenneth Muir, Jay L. Halio, and D. J. Palmer. Newark: U of Delaware P, 1983. 86–97.

Eggers, Walter F., Jr. "Shakespeare's Gower and the Role of the Authorial Presenter." *Philological Quarterly* 54 (1975): 434–43.

Elton, William R. *"King Lear" and the Gods.* San Marino: Huntington Library, 1966.

Erickson, Peter. *Patriarchal Structures in Shakespeare's Drama.* Berkeley: U of California P, 1985.

Ewbank, Inga-Stina. "From Narrative to Dramatic Language: *The Winter's Tale* and Its Source." *Shakespeare and the Sense of Performance.* Ed. Marvin and Ruth Thompson. Newark: U of Delaware P, 1989. 29–47.

Ewbank, Inga-Stina. "The Triumph of Time in *The Winter's Tale.*" *Review of English Literature* 5 (1964): 83–100.

Felperin, Howard. *Shakespearean Romance.* Princeton: Princeton UP, 1972.

Felperin, Howard. "'Tongue-tied Our Queen?': The Deconstruction of Presence in *The Winter's Tale.*" *Shakespeare and the Question of Theory.* Ed. Patricia Parker and Geoffrey Hartman. Methuen: New York, 1985. 3–18.

Foucault, Michel. *The Order of Things.* New York: Vintage, 1973.

Foucault, Michel. "What Is an Author?" *The Foucault Reader.* Ed. Paul Rabinow. New York: Pantheon, 1984. 101–20.

Frey, Charles. *Shakespeare's Vast Romance.* Columbia: U of Missouri P, 1980.

Gower, John. *Confessio Amantis. Complete Works of John Gower.* Ed. G. C. Macaulay. Oxford: Oxford UP, 1901. Vols. 2–3.

Gower, John. *Confessio Amantis. Narrative and Dramatic Sources of Shakespeare.* Ed. Geoffrey Bullough. London: Routledge, 1966. Vol. 6. 375–423.

Greenblatt, Stephen. *Shakespearean Negotiations.* Berkeley: U of California P, 1988.

Greene, Robert. *Pandosto: The Triumph of Time. Narrative and Dramatic Sources of Shakespeare.* Ed. Geoffrey Bullough. London: Routledge, 1975. Vol. 8. 156–99.

Greg, Walter W. "The Date of *King Lear* and Shakespeare's Use of Earlier Versions of the Lear Story." *The Library* 20 (1940): 377–400.

Gurr, Andrew. *Playgoing in Shakespeare's London.* Cambridge: Cambridge UP, 1987.

Haec-Vir. Three Pamphlets on the Jacobean Antifeminist Controversy. Ed. Barbara J. Baines. Delmar: Scholars' Facsimilies, 1978.

Haigh, Christopher. *Elizabeth I.* London: Longman, 1988.

Haigh, Christopher. *English Reformations.* Oxford: Clarendon Press, 1993.

Hibbard, G. R. "*King Lear*: A Retrospect, 1939–79." *Shakespeare Survey* 33 (1980): 1–25.

Hillman, Richard. "Shakespeare's Gower and Gower's Shakespeare: The Larger Debt of *Pericles*." *Shakespeare Quarterly* 36 (1985): 427–37.

Hoeniger, F. D. "Gower and Shakespeare in *Pericles*." *Shakespeare Quarterly* 33 (1982): 461–79.

Hoeniger, F. D., ed. Introduction. *Pericles*. The Arden Shakespeare. London: Methuen, 1963.

Howard, Jean E. "Crossdressing, the Theatre, and Gender Struggle in Early Modern England." *Shakespeare Quarterly* 39 (1988): 418–40.

Jardine, Lisa. *Still Harping on Daughters*. 2nd ed. New York: Columbia UP, 1989.

Jordan, Constance. *Renaissance Feminism*. Ithaca: Cornell UP, 1990.

Kahn, Coppelia. "The Providential Tempest and the Shakespearean Family." *Representing Shakespeare*. Ed. Murray M. Schwartz and Coppelia Kahn. Baltimore: Johns Hopkins UP, 1980. 217–43.

Kelly, Joan. *Women, History, and Theory*. Chicago: U of Chicago P, 1984.

Kimbrough, Robert. "Androgyny Seen Through Shakespeare's Disguise." *Shakespeare Quarterly* 33 (1982): 17–33.

Knight, G. Wilson. "'Great Creating Nature': An Essay on *The Winter's Tale*." *The Crown of Life*. London: Methuen, 1947. 98–128.

Laird, David. "Competing Discourses in *The Winter's Tale*." *Connotations* 4 (1994/95): 25–43.

Law, Robert A. "*King Leir* and *King Lear*: An Examination of the Two Plays." *Studies in Honor of T. W. Baldwin*. Ed. Don C. Allen. Urbana: University of Illinois Press, 1958. 112–24.

Lawlor, John. "*Pandosto* and the Nature of Dramatic Romance." *Philological Quarterly* 41 (1962): 96–113.

Levin, Richard. "Women in the Renaissance Theatre Audience." *Shakespeare Quarterly* 40 (1989): 165–74.

Lodge, Thomas. *Rosalynde. Narrative and Dramatic Sources of Shakespeare*. Ed. Geoffrey Bullough. London: Routledge, 1958. Vol. 2. 158–256.

Loyola, Ignatius. *Spiritual Exercises*. Trans. Charles Seager. London: Dolman, 1847.

Lucretius. *On the Nature of the Universe*. Trans. James H. Mantinband. New York: Frederick Ungar, 1965.

Lyly, John. *Euphues: The Anatomy of Wit. Elizabethan Prose Fiction*. Ed. Merritt Lawlis. New York: Odyssey Press, 1967.

Lynch, Stephen J. "Sin, Suffering, and Redemption in *Leir* and *Lear*." *Shakespeare Studies* 18 (1986): 161–74.

McDonald, Russ. "Poetry and Plot in *The Winter's Tale*." *Shakespeare Quarterly* 36 (1985): 315–29.

McEachern, Claire. "Fathering Herself: A Source Study of Shakespeare's Feminism." *Shakespeare Quarterly* 39 (1988): 269–90.

Mincoff, Marco. "What Shakespeare Did to *Rosalynde*." *Shakespeare Jahrbuch* 96 (1960): 78–89.

Montaigne, Michel de. *Complete Essays of Montaigne*. Trans. Donald M. Frame. Stamford: Stamford UP, 1958.

Montrose, Louis Adrian. "'The Place of a Brother' in *As You Like It*: Social Process and Comic Form." *Shakespeare Quarterly* 32 (1981): 28–54.

Muir, Kenneth. *Sources of Shakespeare's Plays*. New Haven: Yale UP, 1977.

Mullaney, Steven. *The Place of the Stage*. Chicago: U of Chicago P, 1988.

Neely, Carol Thomas. "*The Winter's Tale*: The Triumph of Speech." *Studies in English Literature* 15 (1975): 321–38.

New Variorum Edition of Shakespeare: "As You Like It." Ed. Richard Knowles. New York: Modern Language Association, 1977.

Newman, Karen. *Fashioning Femininity and English Renaissance Drama*. Chicago: U of Chicago P, 1991.

Orgel, Stephen. "The Poetics of Incomprehensibility." *Shakespeare Quarterly* 42 (1991): 431–37.

Palliser, D. M. *The Age of Elizabeth*. London: Longman, 1983.

Perkinson, Richard H. "Shakespeare's Revision of the Lear Story and the Structure of *King Lear*." *Philological Quarterly* 22 (1943): 315–29.

Pierce, Robert B. "The Moral Languages of *Rosalynde* and *As You Like It*." *Studies in Philology* 68 (1971): 167–76.

Plato. *Symposium*. Trans. Walter Hamilton. New York: Penguin, 1951.

Rackin, Phyllis. "Androgyny, Mimesis, and the Marriage of the Boy Heroine on the English Renaissance Stage." *PMLA* 102 (1987): 29–41.

Scarisbrick, J. J. *The Reformation and the English People*. Oxford: Basil Blackwell, 1984.

Schoenbaum, S. *William Shakespeare: A Compact Documentary Life*. Oxford: Oxford UP, 1977.

Semon, Kenneth J. "*Pericles*: An Order Beyond Reason." *Essays in Literature* 1 (1974): 17–27.

Shakespeare, William. *Complete Works of Shakespeare*. Ed. David Bevington. 4th ed. New York: Harper Collins, 1992.

Shakespeare, William. *The History of King Lear* (Quarto text). *William Shakespeare: The Complete Works*. Ed. Stanley Wells and Gary Taylor. Oxford: Clarendon Press, 1986.

Shakespeare, William. *The Tragedy of King Lear* (Folio text). *William Shakespeare: The Complete Works*. Ed. Stanley Wells and Gary Taylor. Oxford: Clarendon Press, 1986.

Sidney, Sir Philip. Selected Prose and Poetry. Ed. Robert Kimbrough. New York: Holt, Rinehart and Winston, 1969.

Smith, Jonathan. "The Language of Leontes."*Shakespeare Quarterly* 19 (1968): 317–27.

Song of Roland. Trans. Robert Harrison. New York: Mentor, 1970.

Spenser, Edmund. *Faerie Queene*. Ed. Thomas P. Roche, Jr. New Haven: Yale UP, 1981.

Stone, Lawrence. *The Family, Sex, and Marriage in England 1500–1800*. New York: Harper and Row, 1977.

Taylor, Gary. *Reinventing Shakespeare*. Oxford: Oxford UP, 1989.

Thomas, Keith. *Religion and the Decline of Magic*. London: Penguin, 1973.

True Chronicle Historie of King Leir and His Three Daughters. Narrative and Dramatic Sources of Shakespeare. Ed. Geoffrey Bullough. London: Routledge, 1973. Vol. 7. 337–402.

Ward, David. "Affection, Intention, and Dreams in *The Winter's Tale*." *MLR* 82 (1987): 545–54.

Williams, Penry. *The Tudor Regime*. Oxford: Clarendon Press, 1979.

Yeager, Robert F. "English, Latin, and the Text as 'Other': The Page as Sign in the Work of John Gower." *Text: Transactions of the Society for Textual Scholarship* 3 (1987): 251–67.

Youings, Joyce. *Sixteenth-Century England*. Harmondsworth: Penguin, 1984.

Index

About the Author

STEPHEN J. LYNCH is Professor of English at Providence College. He has published articles on Shakespeare in scholarly journals such as *Shakespeare Studies*, *Philological Quarterly*, *Mediaevalia*, *The Upstart Crow*, and *South Atlantic Review*. He has also taught at the University of North Carolina at Asheville and at the University of Georgia.

ISBN 0-313-30726-1

90000>

EAN

9 780313 307263

HARDCOVER BAR CODE

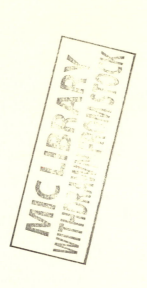